Here Come the Mountainy Men

By the Same Author

Everyday Buildings of Ireland
Shops of Ireland
Ireland and the New Architecture
A Field Guide to the Buildings of Ireland
A Long Walk South
Snow on the Equator

As Editor

Searching: Nuala Rothery, Writings

Here Come the Mountainy Men

A Memoir

Sean Rothery

The Liffey Press

Published by
The Liffey Press Ltd
'Clareville'
307 Clontarf Road
Dublin D03 PO46, Ireland

A catalogue record of this book is
available from the British Library.

ISBN 978-0-9957927-8-4

Printed in Spain by GraphyCems.

Acknowledgements

My first thanks must be to my brother Brian and sister Isobel who were so much part of my early years in our home in Woodside and for their sharing of memories with me. Special thanks also to John and Mary O'Reilly who were fellow students in far-off days in Earlsfort Terrace and who helped with their remembrance of those old architectural studios.

Thanks also to Fiachra O'Brolachain and Cillian de Burca from An Siopa Leabhar.

As the work progressed, Barbara Dowds, Joan Davis and Áine O'Connor generously offered opinions that helped towards insights in the developing story. Finally, as always, I am deeply grateful for the patient advice and meticulous skills of Jonathan Williams as my editor.

For my sister Isobel, brother Brian,
and in fond memory of dear Eamon

Remembering Nuala

'Passion is lord of infinite space, and distant objects please because they border on its confines, and are moulded by its touch.'

William Hazlitt, 'Why Distant Objects Please'

Prelude

The track up the mountain rose steeply at first, but soon levelled off and then looped, easing the contours past overgrown and abandoned quarry holes until the tiny bog meadow appeared. I paused here, remembering. The stream still flowed out of the well behind the big boulder, and grasses and rushes flourished beside the little pools where, as children, we poked at the frogspawn and later collected tadpoles in jam jars. Here and there were clumps of quaking grass, or shivery grass, as we called it. Beside the track a small patch of yellow-flowered stonecrop carpeted a pile of granite chippings, as an old quarry once scooped out a steep face from the hill. Thick furze bushes made it difficult to find a way up the side of the rocky wall, but at the top the ground fell away to a miniature glen. I looked down and just below the lip of the ridge there it was: the 'nook'.

It was a shallow cleft in the rocks, a sloping floor of dense grasses and it faced west, towards the setting sun. I would often come here as a boy, to escape tensions at home or perhaps just to seek solitude in a quiet place. I eased myself down into the narrow space and sat for a while. I had not been here for more than six decades. Had anything changed? The close view was the same: granite, dwarf furze with little yellow blossoms, ferns and heather clumps. The long view was different. Ahead, a fringe of conifers was a foreground to the distant west Dublin hills, but the biggest change was the spreading sea of suburbs, now lapping at the edge of the foothills. It was no longer a quiet place: the unrelenting, if distant, roar of the motorway below was an invasion. It was no place for daydreaming now. I remembered how it was.

I first discovered the nook as a twelve-year-old, roaming the hills, damming the stream, throwing stones in the ponds, shooting arrows from home-made bows, but often settling down in the rocky cleft to read and pass the time in solitary tranquillity. The sounds were different then. Although most of the small quarries had been long abandoned, a few were still worked on the slopes above my home. The tac-tac-tac of the chisels chipping away the dross from the granite blocks being dressed into the windowsills, lintels, quoins, barges and ashlars of Dublin's houses may have been a pervasive sound but it was an oddly reassuring one to me in those days: a cementing of that sense of place when I returned each evening from a city centre school. Samuel Beckett and his father heard these incessant stone-working sounds on their walks here in the 1930s, but Samuel was loftily dismissive of, as he described them, 'the hovels of the stonecutters'. 'Cooldrinagh', the Beckett home in the nearby salubrious suburb of Foxrock, was a millionaire's mansion compared to the little houses of the stonecutters and quarrymen. These were, of necessity, closely clustered along the roadside of Barnacullia, to leave the hillside free for the carving out of the beautiful white granite.

I left the nook and continued up the mountain. It was really only a hill, but to us youngsters in those days it was a mountain. There was another place, higher up, to which I could escape as I grew older and it seemed to offer a suitable refuge from the modern city's dissonance. The nearest summit was scarred with an ugly mess of tall steel masts, antennae, wires and blockhouses, sacrificed to the insatiable demands of the communications industry. I found a flint arrowhead here as a boy, in a small earthwork, now obliterated. I brought it to the National Museum where a curator gravely informed me that it was a testament to Stone Age settlement. It was a bare mountain then, a sea of heather, out of which great granite tors rode the skyline.

A short climb led to the higher summit, crowned with a megalithic burial cairn, as were several of the hills nearby. Two smaller tors sat along the southern shoulder, and one of these had, at its foot, a shallow, grassy depression, facing south, sheltered from the wind: a perfect refuge. I stretched out here and it was if nothing had changed. The only sound was the wind. This was the force that had for millions of years carved the granite of the tor, moulding its rounded bulk into snowdrift form, etching out weak fault lines and creating a texture where the harder quartz stood proud of the feldspar body. It was a quiet place and, when the sun shone, an ideal place to daydream: to remember.

The lane linked the upper road that snaked up along the flanks of the Three Rock Mountain down to the lowlands, as the locals called it. It was not very long: a quarter-mile at most, but for us children on the way to school each morning the journey along this lane was an adventure. It curved and meandered, as if dreaming, before finally joining the sober, undeviating main road below.

The first half sloped steeply downhill and the entry to the lane was cut into the slope with walls of stone holding back the banks. An early curve hid the extent of the fall that ended with a sharp corner. Here was the star turn: the water pump. A fat, black, cast iron column with a lion's head spout and a knurled knob just asking to be turned. Not now, however. School beckoned, but more temptations lay ahead. It was flat going past the little group of cottages that gave the name to Slate Cabin Lane and the curves of the little stream down from the mountain forced the way to follow its twists and turns. The low bank was a temptation to jump over the water into the field but this again had to be resisted, for now at least. The Little Wood came next. It was hardly a wood since it had just a single beech tree, surrounded by a tangle of scrubby thorn bushes and bramble hedges, but it was the only tree on the lane so far and therefore had an important presence.

At last the school building appeared, the front facing the main road and a low wall enclosed the schoolyard. Five tall trees stood at the edges and the stream flowed freely along one side.

I first entered St. Mary's National School aged four, and my memory of the old building was of an open porch where a wooden trapdoor covered a coal-hole. The Infants' classroom was at one end, furnished with rows of wooden benches and presided over by Miss O'Neill. The Low Babies could sit, but the High Infants had to stand. I have very little memory of those early classes with Miss O'Neill but one memory is stark: the 'cursèd teapot', an indelible image from the Art Class. That utensil was taken out once a week and our task was to draw it. Drawing books were handed out, along with pastels: the horrible chalky ones that scratched across the paper when a smooth flowing line from oily ones would have been a pleasure to use. The books had tissue paper between each page and, when time was up, we had to carefully close our book with the tissue paper protecting our work. The books were then handed up and deposited back in the class cupboard until the next week's ordeal.

The old school was demolished in the early 1930s and classes were continued in the Carnegie Library next door. The new building was completed about 1936 and, when we moved back, we were amazed at the bright light of the classrooms after the gloominess of the old building. The girls were upstairs and although we all had to share the same playground, the separation of the sexes was solved by separate playtimes. One memory of the early days in the new school is of the kind of punishments that could be inflicted in those times. A boy was humiliated by being made to stand for hours outside the building, in a corner exposed to the public roadway. To compound his shame and misery, he was forced to wear a petticoat, borrowed from the girls' classes upstairs, over his clothes.

Mr. Greenan had the middle class. He was a slight, shy man, and I have no memory of my time with him as my teacher. The headmaster was Mr. O'Keeffe, a tall, thin man who commanded respect. He lived in Dundrum and on most days would walk up the back road through Ballinteer and then on a rough track over Sheil's Hill, a rounded wilderness where seas of furze were yellow in spring. I have never forgotten the one and only, but remarkable, occasion when Mr. O'Keeffe took our class on a nature walk. It happened to be on the hill just above my house, but that didn't matter, because it was an adventure, unfortunately never to be repeated in any of my future schoolboy years.

I might have been considered a reasonable scholar but one incident in Mr. O'Keeffe's class remains in my memory. The periodic visitation of the *Cigire*, the Department of Education Inspector, was a major and potentially stressful event. He – and it was always a man – would ask questions of the boys and quick and correct answers would be desirable. My desk was near the rear of the class but on the morning of one visit, Mr. O'Keeffe ordered me to move up to the front row. When the great man arrived, he directed all the questions to me. I must have answered correctly when the Inspector turned to chat with the headmaster and then left. That afternoon Mr. O'Keeffe presented me with a geometry set: a splendidly coloured tin box containing a shiny compass, dividers, a protractor and a steel ruler. I loved it but wondered, decades later, was there an arrangement between the Inspector and the headmaster? It was surely a set-up.

In the new school the playground was levelled, properly surfaced and the stream was covered over in a conduit, thus removing one source of adventure at playtime. We could, in the past, throw stones into the water, splash and, if we were older than the infants, tell stories about water rats lurking in the stream and huge ones in the dark of the coal-hole of the old school. The new playground was taken over by the ball-playing boys, and those of us who did not relish being kicked, pushed, tackled and shouted at kept strictly to the edges and out of the way of strife.

We always called him Blacky. I don't know why, since his face was more ruddy than dark, but he had a purplish stain on one cheek that may have been the trigger for his nickname. He would stand, during playtime, under one of the sycamores forming the northern boundary of the schoolyard. He just stood there: I never remember him taking part in any of the activities in the yard. He was big – by far the biggest boy in our class – and he always had an expression of bewilderment, as if he did not know what to expect next but whatever it was to be, it would be bad. He was slow and was often punished for this in class. I never remember Blacky being bullied and he was certainly too passive, despite his size, to do anything but be there, day after day, in silence. He often seemed to have a little group around him while he almost towered above them, like a totem, beside the well-polished trunk of that old sycamore. I could never understand how I could retain that image of Blacky for all those years. Was it compassion? Perhaps. Could I have felt such an emotion as a seven- or eight-year-old? Who knows, but maybe it was simply a sense of relief that I, at least, did not stand out from the noisy crowd as such a lonely figure.

After I left St. Mary's I never saw Blacky again, or heard what had happened to him. I never even knew his proper name, but his image has stayed in my memory: that unhappy face staring out at nobody and at nothing in particular.

The journey home from school could take quite a while: there were so many distractions along the way. First came the little wood where, in season, beechnuts covered the road and they had to be sampled. Then came the turnip field. Again in season, a quick and furtive raid could snatch a nice sweet trophy to be gnawed all the way home, but then, at the bottom of the steep lane, the pump stopped all progress. When you turned that knurled knob, the water could suddenly belch out, splashing everybody standing near and drenching shoes and socks. The trouble this would cause at home could be postponed, for a while at least, because the necessity of trying to drink from the spout was paramount. Distractions were still not over because near the top of the lane there was the possibility of a wren's nest in the deep crevices of stonewalls. In season, the bushy hazel clumps on top of the field wall could yield some delicious nuts before we faced the inevitable parental wrath. 'Why are you so late? Just look at those wringing wet shoes.'

It was my mother's idea that I must be an altar boy. It certainly wasn't mine. Most of all, I did not look forward to the very early starts. It was a mid-winter morning for my first appearance and my walk down to Sandyford Church was in deep dark for early Mass. I still remember taking the short cut across the pastures where puddles of water were frozen, and it was satisfying to crunch and crackle the ice all the way to the little stream that still flowed past the side of the church. The tiny sacristy was quite warm and my first impression was the amount of congealed candle grease that clung to every counter surface. The head altar boy handed me my new uniform – a black soutane that I immediately hated. It was heavy and stiff and felt horrible when I pulled it over my head. The surplice was an improvement, sparkling white and freshly laundered, with a lace hem.

It was a nervous moment waiting for the door to the altar to open, but when we all walked out in solemn procession it was a new experience to feel special and part of something important. There were often six altar boys, three on each side, and the best time was during the sermon when we were allowed, instead of kneeling, to loll back on the steps and gaze at the congregation. I never got to light the candles but this was a highly sought after solo performance. I was, however, sometimes asked to quench the lights after Mass was over: an interesting task, using a long pole and a cup-shaped top. Everybody was leaving at that stage, so my performance was usually ignored. I never got to ring the altar bell, but most of all I never qualified to swing the thurible at Benediction and spread around that wonderful incense aroma. My career as an altar boy did not last very long because the important roles were jealously monopolised and a new entrant took my place. My younger brother Eamon's career was even shorter because in his first few days he kept moving to the wrong side of the altar and was duly sacked. I don't remember that either of us felt let down.

Woodside was a somewhat disjointed townland. It consisted mostly of lands on either side of the Slate Cabin Lane, which meant that some of it was in the lowlands and some on the upper road. A much more coherent place was Barnacullia, a short distance up from Woodside. This was the stonecutters' village where the only logic in its layout was that it straggled along both sides of the road, with the mountain, pockmarked with quarry holes, on the upper side, while the fields on the lower side swept down to the splendour of Fernhill, known as Walker's Wood, after the owner. The Three Rock Mountain dominated all. It was the source of the main employment at the time, with three main quarries and numerous small enterprises along the eastern slopes. These were small excavations into the bedrock to expose the unblemished core granite that could then be wedged and split out into great rough blocks. In the main quarries the more skilled craftsmen would dress, shape and sculpt the stone into the granite ashlars, quoins, lintels, voussoirs, transoms, mullions, barges, consoles, finials and all the myriad stone elements that interlock and form to make architecture. One of the higher quarries was notable for its spectacularly white granite that would sparkle in sunshine. It, of course, became the stone of choice for the new St Mary's School, but the granite from the quarry later became a precious mine for sculptors.

Many of the old quarry holes became disused when the core solid granite fragmented and the excavation gradually filled up with water. There was one small one directly above our house which was a perfect playground for my brothers and me. A larger quarry not far above was still being actively worked, although the core stone in the main excavated section was long exhausted and a fresh gash was now opened into one side. The old hole filled up with water and was quite deep. It became a favourite swimming hole for local youngsters and featured a steep, smooth, rock slab down which divers could race, whooping, into the deep. This was Malone's Pond.

My early schoolboy wanderings led to a fascination with the machinery and engines of the stone industry. The tripod hoists, steel cranes, all often abandoned and rusty, were enticing objects for drawing, particularly when located against the rocky quarry walls and fern-covered stone detritus. I usually steered clear of the working places since I was ordered off once just before blasting commenced. Here, open sheds with corrugated iron roofs sheltered the craftsmen who dressed the stones into the finished units, while roaring braziers were kept blazing hot with bellows, to sharpen the cutting tools. Times were often hard when contracts for cut and shaped granite elements were scarce; at the worst of times there was no work at all in the quarries. Emigration was the only way to make a living, and so many of the craftsmen of Barnacullia took the boats to Holyhead or Liverpool. There were two great cathedrals being built in Liverpool at the time and these needed great numbers of stone workers. The Irish were a large contingent in the workforce. The Roman Catholic cathedral was designed by Sir Edwin Lutyens but work on it ceased after the beautiful crypt was finished. The building was not completed until well into the twentieth century. Gilbert Scott designed the Protestant cathedral in the Neo-Gothic style and it was a great work needing an enormous supply of stone detailing. My father recalled that as a boy he remembered workers from Barnacullia walking down to Dun Laoghaire (at that time Kingstown) to the mail boat for work in England. Many, he said, carried their own tools, hammers and chisels, wrapped in brown paper. One old man, he remembered, openly carried in his hand his lump hammer.

Some of the quarrymen who stayed at home would carve pieces for their own pleasure. Two elderly men from Woodside told me about their favourite decorative pieces; a bunch of grapes was one of the most difficult, as was a stone pineapple. The most challenging of all, however, was to carve a large, perfectly spherical granite ball. This would be a triumph. Stone granite balls were often desired as capping for gateposts.

Our house may have been only seven miles from the city centre but the entire neighbourhood was rural. The near view from our house was of green fields stretching for miles to the suburb of Foxrock. Even close to this affluent and bosky place there were farms. One of my uncles had a dairy at nearby Cabinteely. He would sometimes take us children on one of his rounds in his horse-drawn milk float. I have a strong memory of the pair of polished brass taps at the rear and the foaming and fresh smelling filling of customers' jugs.

The large farm below us was Lenehans and the fields just in front of our house were a source of endless pleasure to me, as well as founts of free food. The end of summer was blackberry-picking time and there was always a competition to get at the 'lobbers', as we called them – the biggest, fattest and juiciest ones, often high up and nearly inaccessible. My mother was an expert at making blackberry jam and the empty jars from the previous year were soon refilled. Mushroom time came later in the autumn and we became adept at finding the best spots for these treasures. The small button ones were ideal, and threading each find through a strong grass stalk was a mark of expertise and pride. Early morning was the perfect time for picking and the reward was a delicious breakfast when we returned from the dew-drenched fields.

Haymaking was in early summer. The long-grass meadows were mown, usually in June, and the green grass was left to dry before being tossed up into separate piles and allowed to mature. These haycocks were dotted as light yellow domes in the surrounding fields. The local farmer was indulgent to us children during this special time of saving the hay. It was an exciting day when the hay bogies arrived to take the precious fodder to the barns. These were flat wooden platforms, pulled by horses, and when the contraption was tilted and inserted under the edge of the haycock, the whole dome would be ratcheted up onto the levelled-out bogie. We were allowed to climb up onto the hay and enjoy the ride back down to the hayshed. The return trip was a different experience. The bogie was now a glistening platform, polished to a glassy slipperiness by the years of hay friction. It was a giddy delight to hang on up the Slate Cabin Lane, trying not to slip off.

The fields in summer were something of a secret pleasure for me in those far-off days. Natural history was always a passion but when I built up a small library of little guides to everything from wild flowers, grasses, ferns, birds and wildlife, the collecting bug grew. The grasses of the meadows were an immediate attraction and attempting to identify each species appealed to my explorer instincts. The names were fascinating: crested dog's-tail, perennial rye grass, creeping bent and, best of all, sweet vernal grass. The guidebook stated that this beautifully named grass was the source of the sweet-smelling scent of new-mown hay. I tried to find an example of each one and then, following instructions, pressed them dry between two sheets of absorbent paper. The specimens then could be mounted in a scrapbook.

The sheer beauty of those meadows of early summer touched me as a boy, and the memory of them has stayed fresh for a lifetime. An inspiring English teacher introduced me to the poetry of Francis Ledwidge and especially his early series *Songs of Spring*. My favourite poem in the series was 'June'.

The hedges are all drowned in green grass seas,
And bobbing poppies flare like Elmor's light
While siren-like the pollen-stainèd bees
Drone in the clover depths. And up the height
The cuckoo's voice is hoarse and broke with joy.
And on the lowland crops the crows make raid,
Nor fear the clappers of the farmer's boy,
Who sleeps, like drunken Noah, in the shade.

The meadows below our house in early summer were certainly sea-like, when the wind sent green grass waves flowing across the surface of the fields. The long grasses had myriad shades of green, and wildflowers speckled colour all through the lushness. The two fields below our house had corncrakes when the meadows were deep in long grass and their harsh call, 'kerrx-kerrx', is now only a fading memory.

Snow in almost every winter was wildly welcomed, and the steeply sloping fields became a new playground. We could swoop down on home-made toboggans or, more dangerously and certainly faster, on sheets of old corrugated iron where the front was bent up and with a string for steering attached. A really fast run could end with us crashing into the lower hedge, then the long trudge back up the hill before endless repeats. We would come home as darkness fell, exhausted and wet through from melting snow, and hope for no school in the morning.

My paternal grandmother, Isabella, had a little green field on the lower slopes of the Three Rock Mountain. It was hardly more than two acres and was bounded on all four sides by ancient stone walls. The rear boundary was actually a retaining wall against the steep slope of the wilder mountain, an area of granite quarry holes and deep thickets of furze. It was crowned by a hedgerow of holly and brambles with a few thorn trees that blossomed white in early spring. It was here that my father built our house on the one-third of the field given to him by his mother. The actual builder was my uncle John Hayden, but my father had fairly quickly added some extensions to the neat three-roomed bungalow, the work of the more professional Uncle John. The extensions consisted of a flat-roofed dining room, a kitchen and a bathroom.

A tiny scullery led out from the kitchen to a shed. This was a crudely built structure that, nevertheless, became a wonderful place of work and pleasure for me. It consisted of a lean-to at the rear of the house and was constructed with old window frames, forming the walls on all three sides, and one side frame containing a door to the outside. The shed was then roofed with corrugated iron sheets. Since the sides were each fully glazed, it was a marvellously day-lit space but, best of all, on sunny days it was warm and I felt that it became my own sunroom. My growing hobby of fretwork and model-making was now engaging me more and more. Most of the space was taken up by a large ancient workbench, made of heavy baulks of timber, blackened and scarred by years of use. It had a bolted-on iron vice at one end that was ideal for my fretwork-shaping. My father was a great smoker, and one of the first items I made for him was an elaborately ornate pipe rack. I'm sure it must have been a horrible object to me later, in my early years as an arrogant and minimalist architecture student.

A stray dog moved into the shed late one evening. He had come from somewhere in the near neighbourhood where he was unwanted and certainly unloved. He was a Kerry Blue, old and unkempt, with rheumy eyes and a graying muzzle, and we called him Sykie. We put down some old overcoats as a bed and he settled in a corner of the shed, out of the way. He rarely left his bed. Whenever we brought him his food, he would look up with those old eyes and his stump of a tail would give a spasmodic wag. We had other dogs at the time but they generally ignored Sykie, seeing him as no threat or, perhaps, as a venerable old dog that deserved respect. When we brought his food one morning, his bed was empty. He must have gone away to die, we thought.

My brother Eamon got a chemistry set from Santa one Christmas and he used the shed for his chemistry experiments. He made a bomb and the explosion nearly blew the roof off. It was easy to fix the sheets of corrugated iron back in place and Eamon just suffered a blackened face. He went on to be a scientist and the head of a college Chemistry Department.

To emphasise my father's early embrace of the motorcar, for business as well as pleasure, he added a garage. It had a new-fangled sliding and folding door that never, to my memory, worked properly but would stick in its tracks or jump out entirely. The flat roofs constantly leaked in rainy weather and, in my mother's words, became 'a cross I will always have to bear'. The year was 1930 and our house was one of the first new houses to appear at the northern end of the stonecutters' village. The house name was painted on the wooden gate and, as the only new house on the road, it was called 'Woodside', after the townland.

My grandmother's house was older. It was two-storey and only a short distance from our home. One of my earliest memories was of Grandmother Isabella, in a long black dress, standing at her front door, looking very severe. She had a flock of white geese, and no dog could hope to slink past her gate before the birds, wings outstretched and hissing angrily, chased away the intruder. The house was built tightly up against an old quarry wall and had a tiny rear yard, which got little sun, especially in winter. It seems to have been a 'safe house' during the War of Independence, or the Black and Tan War as my father sometimes called it. Two of the children of prominent nationalist Desmond FitzGerald, later a cabinet minister in the newly formed Free State, were hidden here when their father was on the run from British forces.

My paternal grandfather, John, was born in 1848 and died aged just fifty-four, in 1901. There seems to be no family memories of him at all, except that he was buried in the old graveyard in Glencullen. He is listed in the Census of 1901 with the occupation 'farmer' and that he could 'read only'. My grandmother was a widow at forty-five and in the 1911 census she is listed as 'Head of Family'. My father, Thomas, was the youngest of the family, with four older sisters and two older brothers. My aunts, Margaret, Kathy, Mary and Nan, all married and had separate families while my father was still a boy. The older brother, William, was killed at the age of twenty in a horse and cart accident and he had been one of the wage-earners in the household. My Uncle Mick, two years older than my father, was a postman at eighteen and my father was a telegraph messenger with his age listed as sixteen. There was a boarder, named James Dwyer, and he also worked, so it seems to have been a very industrious household.

My father was born in 1895 and I often wondered if this early job was a forecast of his later work ethic and a foundation for his subsequent life as an entrepreneur: a life that was to be a sequence of both success and failure. He rarely spoke of his experiences in those violent years between 1916 and 1922, but when I asked him once he told me that, as a twenty-year-old he had tried to get into Dublin in 1916 to join the Rising, but, along with other young men from Barnacullia, he was stopped by the British Army at Milltown Bridge and sent home. He told me little about his time in the Old IRA during the War of Independence. Many years later, however, a couple of photographs from an old collection were, perhaps, windows into the story of those times. The earliest one showed a group of young men, casually posed, with some sitting and others standing against a wall outside the Blue Light pub in Barnacullia. They are each named as locals, except two who remain unnamed, and the photograph is entitled 'The Barnacullia IRA in 1919'. No one is armed or at least no guns are visible, but most of the lads are smiling and, although they are somewhat dishevelled-looking in their everyday and ill-fitting clothes, they have a devil-may-care air about them. My father is one of them. He would have been about twenty-two. Another photo shows a more organised and definitely military scenario. The scene is probably Fulham's Glen, on the slopes of Three Rock Mountain. There is a tent and beside it a neat vertical stack of rifles. An unidentified man is soberly and neatly dressed and has an ammunition bandolier slung across his shoulder and chest.

My father never spoke of the subsequent Civil War. I do, however, have a strong memory of being brought, as a young child in the early 1930s, to a ceremony on the Featherbed in the Dublin Mountains. I remember playing in the heather with other small children while the adults gathered around a monument. My father never explained what this was about and it was only in far later years that I realised that this was where Noel Lemass, a prominent fighter in the anti-Treaty forces in the Civil War, had been assassinated.

My mother Mary's maiden name was Gaffney and she grew up in the old village of Windy Arbour. There were family stories that she and my father knew each other at the time of the War of Independence. It seems unlikely that the 'Roaring Twenties' would have had much of a sartorial effect on my parents to be, as studio photos of the time indicate. One photo shows my mother sitting primly in an antique chair, wearing a sedate, below the knee skirt and a serious blouse. No flapper dress here, but who knows, she possibly had one at home. My father stands stiffly behind, one hand on the back of my mother's chair and looking uncomfortable in a formal suit. An artificial palm tree behind the pair completes this stilted portrait. They do look good, however. My father is a handsome devil and my mother is beautiful.

I don't think my mother was ever really happy living in Woodside. She always felt that she was an outsider, now compelled to live in the Dublin Mountains. The wilderness was on our doorstep; the little houses straggled along the slopes in no coherent order; the gravel road snaked upwards without any apparent destination in mind but, above all, an absence of street lights. The nights were black. Winter was worse, with deep snow in almost every one of those early years in Woodside. There was no electricity and my mother found the lighting of oil lamps slow and messy. Windy Arbour was really only a village in those years but it was in the lowlands and was close to the outer suburbs of the city. This was a factor, at least in her eyes. that made it a far more refined place than the quarrymen's jumble of houses on the barren slopes of Three Rock Mountain.

Leaving her best friend, Ciss Seawright, behind was most probably the real reason for my mother's initial unhappiness at the move to Woodside. Their close friendship was to last a lifetime. Mrs Seawright and her husband lived just outside the village of Dundrum, in a little gate lodge. When my mother married, she and my father moved into another little gate lodge in the nearby neighbourhood of Roebuck. There were few houses in that scattered place and it was only a short walk from one to the other. The two couples were much the same age and it was natural, I suppose, that they became friends.

It was interesting, however, because Mrs Seawright and her husband were Belfast Protestants and my mother and father were conventional Roman Catholics. Religion, it seemed, was no barrier.

The neighbourhood of Dundrum and Roebuck was a world apart from the mountain villages of Woodside and Barnacullia. It was an old and settled one, with a definite air of self-satisfied gentility. The gate lodge was not the guardian of a great mansion but rather a statement of the importance of the owners of the main house. These were usually from the professional class or successful business people. The lodge my parents lived in for those few years while our eventual house in Woodside was being built was called Dromartin Lodge and it was attached to a larger house that belonged to a doctor. I have a vivid memory of that lodge and the garden of the main house. I can't have been much older than two. I am allowed to pick up apples from the orchard and carry them home. I have them clutched in my arms. The apples are big and some keep falling, but it was huge adventure.

Mr. and Mrs. Seawright's garden, which I visited frequently, remains the most memorable. It was a tiny space, walled in by the lodge on one side and by high granite walls on two sides and dense rhododendron bushes on the fourth side. It was more like a clearing in a forest. The garden may have been small but to me, as a ten-year-old, it was another world and far from the windy slopes of Three Rock Mountain. All my memories are of hot summer days, of drowsy afternoons, insects buzzing and an overwhelming lushness of growing things. There were lines of fat marrows, glistening, round cabbages and so many other vegetables that were new to me. It was, however, the sheer abundance of fruits that delighted me most. The pears, draped on their branches spread out on the sunlit granite walls, were a temptation, but picking was forbidden. Mr Seawright I remember as a tall, if stooped, figure and always with a wide-brimmed hat, and he kindly explained to me that we had to wait for the pears to be properly ripened before picking. There were redcurrants, blackcurrants and raspberries, but it was the loganberries that have remained in my memory. The bushes were head height to me and I was allowed to pick my fill of those huge, deep crimson berries that slid easily off their white stems.

Dundrum, quite a small village in those days, was my mother's favourite place for shopping. The venerable grocery shop Leverett and Frye, on the corner of the main street, was the source of most of our food. Visits there with my mother, when my brothers Eamon and Brian and little sister Isobel and I were children, were always a joy. I remember, as if it were yesterday, two wonders that inevitably fascinated me. The first was the biscuit display. Under the main counter, a row of opened tins were arranged, showing the most delectable variety of offerings. A selection could be made, carefully wrapped in tissue, and popped into a stout brown paper bag. The best and unique wonder was, however, the aerial transport of money. When you paid over the counter, the cash and invoice were placed in a little brass capsule that was pulled down from a lacework of overhead wires. The capsule was then shot at lightning speed along the ceiling wires to a small upper cubicle. Behind a glass window a figure sat. In my mind this was a God-like person who collected all the money and then sent back, also at speed, receipts and sometimes change. She, and it was usually a she, must be very rich, I thought.

Tom Turner was the van man for the grocer's and he would do a delivery to Woodside once a week. He lived in a small cottage on the Sandyford Road and he too was an expert gardener.

His vegetable garden was famous and sometimes my mother would order produce from him. Tom worked for Leverett and Frye for many years. After his retirement he lived and worked in his beloved garden well into his nineties. He was a stalwart of the Kilternan Country Market, one of the country's first.

The sweet shop came next. It must have sold more than sweets and chocolate, but all I remember were the sweets, and especially the chocolate. The owners, two old ladies (at least to my child's eye), must have been long-time friends of my mother, because she usually had interminable conversations with them while we were itching to go home and enjoy our delights. The window of this shop on the main street was an Aladdin's cave: a cornucopia of chocolate bars and boxes, in a seductive riot of colours. Cadbury was always my first choice. Flake was sheer ecstasy; it would melt in your mouth but would never last long. Dairy Milk, Aero, Fruit and Nut could last for ages if you nibbled them, square by square. It was a shock to us children when one of the old ladies said that the window display chocolates were actually just slabs of wood inside those wonderful wrappers. She gave us, however, a bundle of these false bars that she said we could include in our play shop at home. This sounded like a great idea and we looked forward to fooling our friends with such a tempting display. We did.

In complete contrast to my father, my mother was a great reader. I have no doubt that books gave her great consolation when she moved up from her beloved lowlands to the wild and rugged mountain, which is how she regarded Woodside. She was a lover of romantic fiction and I always remember her saying that Daphne du Maurier was one of her much-loved authors, *Rebecca* being a popular book at the time. Ethel M. Dell, another writer of romantic fiction, was a name she often mentioned, as were A.J. Cronin and Somerset Maugham.

Maugham's *Of Human Bondage* and *The Moon and Sixpence* were widely read in the 1930s and '40s. Most of all I remember J. B. Priestley's *Angel Pavement*. This was one of a handful of old books that remained in the house, then named 'Woodside', long after my mother died. I read this story when my wife Nuala and I came to live in 'Woodside' shortly after my mother moved away, from a house that was cold and damp, and where the roofs continually leaked.

Priestley's novel remained one of my own favourites and I must have reread it several times over the years. The character who delighted me most in that simple but beautifully crafted story was Mr Smeeth. Herbert Norman Smeeth was the chief clerk of a small, struggling firm dealing in wood veneers for the furniture trade. He was old-fashioned, a diligent and exacting keeper of the account books, but most of all he was a thoroughly contented man, living a life of undeviating routine. This changed for him in an explosive way when leaving one evening after work. He regularly passed by a concert hall on his way home, without paying particular attention to any advertised programme there. In an act of uncharacteristic spontaneity, he bought a ticket and settled into his first classical music concert ever. It was the Brahms 4th symphony that captivated him, a composer he had only vaguely heard of. From the first dreamy and searching themes he was electrified, right down to the majestic rolling drums of the finale. He left the hall uplifted but somehow disturbed. His life up to that moment was settled and unchanged but now, as he hummed the haunting melodies, he knew that something in him had changed for ever.

My mother had a nephew who was only a few years younger than she was. His name was Tim Mulhall and he worked in the National Library and in the National Museum: both institutions book-ended Leinster House, the Irish Parliament. Tim lived in Monkstown, and at least once a month on his half-day off work he walked up to visit my mother in 'Woodside'. Their mutual interest in books was the main reason given for their meetings, but I think that my mother liked the company of a kindred spirit. She certainly must have been lonely at times, particularly with my father's increasing absences. She also thought of herself as something of a rebel, or at least not totally conforming to the accepted norms of the time. In her late seventies she moved into a retirement home, run by nuns, and while reasonably contented there, she still liked to see herself as that rebel or nonconformist. I always remember her telling my siblings and me about the couple who in their sixties decided to move into the home where, as my mother quoted them as stating, 'We wanted to be able to attend two masses every day.' Mother then said scornfully, 'I only go once a week or maybe twice.' There was a barb barely hidden in that statement. I think she was aware that we had stopped going to mass many years past.

I have a fantasy about my mother. I see her as lying languidly on a chaise longue, smoking expensive Balkan Sobranie cigarettes: these, of course, in a long and elegant holder. She has a half-opened romantic novel on the low table beside her, alongside that box of chocolates that her lover has just left for her. She must at times, wistfully perhaps, have imagined herself as that pampered woman. Sadly, it was never to be and 'Woodside' remained her home for more than three decades.

My mother's favourite brother was my Uncle Joe. He was the youngest of the family and it was, undoubtedly, his romantic nature that so appealed to her. She often spoke of him in nostalgic and loving terms. Joe ran away from home at sixteen to join the British Army; he gave his age as eighteen. He had the romantic vision of being a cavalryman, with plumed helmet and lance, charging the enemy. It was 1914 and the reality for him was a dull khaki uniform, a tin helmet and a rifle. Instead of the North West Frontier of India, he was sent to the Western Front in France. He was almost at once in the retreat from Mons and was at least spared the subsequent horror of the trenches. His parents notified the authorities about his actual age and he was sent home, only to soon take off again and join the Merchant Navy. This time he made his first mature decision and went to train as one of the early Marconi wireless operators. He qualified, achieving his lifelong ambition of world travel. His diaries, although mainly terse and matter-of-fact, with the very bald listing of the places visited in his tramp steamer voyages – Cape Town, Suez, Shanghai, Bombay, Valparaiso, Buenos Aires – spoke of romance and adventure. An intriguing fragment of one diary revealed the closeness of that brotherhood of early ship's wireless operators. He spoke of a visit to the Grand Harbour of Valetta in Malta and having dinner with the Marconi man on the Royal Navy battleship *HMS Ramillies*. Joe was ice-bound in the Gulf of St Lawrence, and during the winter of the early 1930s contracted Bright's Disease and died soon afterwards. My mother frequently spoke in sorrow at the loss of her beloved young brother, as she related stories of his short and colourful life.

Whenever our Uncle Jem wheeled his bicycle up our drive-way in the 1930s, it was an exciting time for my siblings and me. It wasn't just his carbide lamp, with its distinctly sharp smell, or his brightly polished black leather leggings that charmed us. It was the encyclopaedias. He had a whole set of them and each time he came to visit he would bring one volume for us to borrow. Jem was mother's oldest brother and, though he was always welcome, there seemed to be some secret about him.

My mother did tell me once, as if it was somewhat shameful, that Jem was unemployed and a member of the Mount Street Club. This was an organisation that had its members involved in various useful work projects – vegetable-growing being one – which could be part of a bartering scheme. Uncle Jem was a natural gardener. He spent most mornings of his visits working away at converting our back garden into a cornucopia of fruit and vegetables. I have a vivid memory of a small plot of mushrooms that he cultivated, and it must have been Jem who gave us the orchard. This consisted of fourteen apple trees, each one a different variety. I remember only a few names: Bramley and Cox's Orange Pippin, and who could forget Beauty of Bath?

The unspoken secret may have been that after a good morning's work Uncle Jem would disappear, up Ryan's Hill, to the Blue Light pub. My mother's disapproval was noticeable when, after his lunchtime drinking, poor Jem wheeled his bicycle, often unsteadily, until he mounted and rode down the road for the long trip back to the city.

Her disapproval, however, did not extend to her appreciation of his transformation of our garden and the abundance of fresh produce it gave us. She decided one day that each of us children would be given a small piece of garden in which to grow whatever we liked. My plot was close to the boundary of Uncle Mick's field and I decided that, as well as the redcurrant bush already there, in season laden with delicious fruit, I would plant a tree.

A secret place to explore for us had long been Fitzsimons' Wood. We were never sure if we were trespassing when we climbed over the stone wall and sneaked into the shelter of a dense thicket. I remember the cherry trees and, most of all, the Beech Walk, an overgrown and abandoned formal feature, perhaps, of an old and vanished estate. I didn't tell anyone what I had in mind; it was a guilty secret and I knew my mother would disapprove. I intended to steal or, in my conscience at least, liberate a young tree. I slipped over the wall and headed to a large ash that I knew well. All around it were little saplings sprouting up in heights varying from tiny to tall and flourishing specimens. I chose one minute and vigorous plant, dug deeply around its tenacious roots, placed it in a paper bag and sneaked away. I planted it carefully in my own patch and hoped that it would grow to equal its huge parent tree. It was wartime and shortly after my guilty raid the whole wood was devastated: all the trees were felled and salvaged for winter fuel. It was a sad sight, but I was glad that one tree, at least, would survive. It would be *my* ash tree.

One early expedition did not have a very pleasant end. I had started to explore away from 'Woodside' and Three Rock Mountain. Christmas presents of bicycles made this easier for my brothers and me. Isobel was still a toddler when I proposed to the other two that we seek out new territory in County Wicklow. The Scalp was to be our goal: an extraordinary defile, a relic of the Ice Age. We had often passed through it in my father's car when he took us for drives, and I for one could not wait to scramble up those great boulder-strewn slopes to reach the top.

The cycle ride was easy, and when we arrived at the northern end of the gorge we hid our bikes behind a stone wall. It was exciting to clamber up the sunlit side, meandering between the massive granite boulders and pine trees, until we came out on to the very lip of the gorge. There was a wide view to the south, dominated by the sharp cone of the Sugarloaf Mountain. I resolved there and then that the ascent of this magical-looking peak would be one of our next adventures. The early bright sunshine had vanished, as we carefully scrambled back down to the road. There was a rising wind, dark clouds boiling up from the west and a far-off rumble of thunder.

We had just pedalled up the road from the Scalp when a torrential thunderstorm and a deluge of rain caught us out. At the summit of the hill, and before the long downhill ride to Kilternan, there were several densely foliaged evergreen trees, just behind a high old wall: an ideal shelter. We settled down here, where the tree canopy provided excellent cover from the relentless downpour. After a few minutes we saw a large group of cyclists pelting up the hill and rushing to join us under the trees. They were all boys and each was dressed in black trousers, jacket and shoes. They were clerical students, aged about sixteen. We were used to seeing large groups of black-clad students in Woodside. On week-day mornings a long file would walk, two by two, up the Slate Cabin Lane, and then the mountain track to the Three Rock summit.

The students soon surrounded my brothers and me, jostling and pushing to get well under the sheltering trees. I was twelve, Eamon was about ten and Brian was maybe seven. I certainly felt hemmed in and did not like being there. It was as if we were being lorded over and I was anxious for the rain to stop so we could escape.

Two of the group, obviously older than the others and apparently the leaders, pushed their way close to where my brothers and I were sheltering. One of them focused on me and said, in a bossy tone, 'Young man, what is your name?'

'Sean.'

'Sean what?'

'Sean Rothery.'

'Sean Rothery what?' he said this in a louder voice.

'Just Sean Rothery.'

This seemed to really annoy him and then I realised what was going on. He wanted me to address him as 'Father'.

'Where do you live?'

He said this after a pause and in a less aggressive tone, but I was getting stubborn and decided not to play his game.

'Woodside,' I said, innocently I thought.

'Woodside what?'

He nearly shouted this and some of the others crowding around started to snigger.

'Sandyford.'

I think that he had had enough at this stage, but he looked unsure about trying further to assert his authority. I was beginning to regret my impertinence and was more than a little fearful. After all, I was used to deference to teachers, who could whack you for being cheeky.

Fortunately the rain eased off, and my tormentor ordered his group to set off down the hill. My brothers did not say anything and I waited until the clerical bunch disappeared down the long road to Kilternan. When we pedalled off, I, at first, felt a sense of triumph that I had bested this bully. I had often seen bullies in action in school. My elation did not last long, however, and deep down I was shaken, and realised that I had been intimidated.

Those evergreen trees, now even more overhanging, are still there behind the high wall. I often drive past, and on most occasions I remember that incident all those years ago. It may have been a trivial one, but the memory of it remains in my psyche.

Winter nights were dark in Woodside. Below and to the north, the city was a compact blaze of light in a surrounding sea of darkness. Electricity came late to our place but my father's energy and enterprise brought us into the modern world, at least for a short while. We got a windmill. It was an American model, called a Wincharger, and it worked fine when a good wind was blowing. A calm day was a different matter, for then the lights would flicker and it was back to the oil lamps. Experiments were made with wet batteries to store the current but it was a big relief, particularly to my mother, when the ESB finally arrived and the townlands of Woodside and Barnacullia now showed ribbons of light all along the flanks of Three Rock Mountain.

My father's main enterprise in those early years between the two world wars was the motor trade. I have vivid memories of his garage in Stillorgan and the two old-fashioned petrol pumps on the roadside. It was a Shell station with the yellow Shell sign on top of the clear glass petrol dispensers. I was sometimes allowed to help hand-crank fuel to customers or to find tins of oil inside the office. The building had a very narrow front to its deep and cluttered interior, and a small wooden counter at a right angle to the window facing the road. There was a large black and white map of Ireland on the wall on which the main monastic sites were marked. The title on the map was 'Ireland. Land of Saints and Scholars'. It was a much older cousin who crossed out the title and replaced it with 'Ireland. Land of Liars and Robbers'. I think I must have been too young to see this as funny or indeed as satire but it has remained in my memory as an affront. It didn't seem to bother my father or his secretary, always known as Miss Grace. She sat behind the wooden counter and I never remember seeing her smile. The much larger service and workshop part of the enterprise was separate from the petrol station and was a far more adventurous place in which to explore. An extensive yard with work sheds at one end was situated at the rear of a row of little cottages. The open part of the yard was filled with an extraordinary and riotous mass of tangled wreckage: old cars and lorries heaped one upon the other, like a nightmare world of Armageddon. For me, however, as a young boy, it was the macabre nature of the scene that drew me to stand there, for a very short while anyway, fearful in the midst of that silent devastation.

The garage was only one part of my father's work domain in those far-off days. He had a small fleet of lorries and rented a sand and gravel pit in Enniskerry. My Uncle Mick was installed there, in a little hut, where he supervised the excavation and washing of the materials before the lorries were loaded and sent off to various destinations. We were allowed to visit occasionally, but it was the walnut tree beside the entrance to the pit that was the main attraction, at least in the autumn when we could climb it and pick the delicious nuts.

My father loved guns. He kept a double-barrelled shotgun in a corner of my parents' bedroom and we were always warned not to touch it. I have a vague memory, as a small boy, of being taken on one of his shooting trips. It was probably to a wetland in Wicklow and the talk was of bagging duck. I remember only the early-morning numbing cold and the boredom of seemingly hours of standing still with nothing happening. I have one enduring memory of that hunting trip, however, and that is the far-off, wistful call of a curlew. Whenever I hear it now, I can see that flat winter tableau: dark waters and speckled reedbeds. It was a lonely cry that stays with me still. My father never tried to pressure me into taking up hunting. I did, however, persuade myself once that such an activity was possibly more appropriate for boys than my solitary and somewhat secretive hobby of collecting and pressing grasses and wildflowers.

I 'borrowed' the shotgun one morning, without permission, and set out on my own first hunting expedition. I was about thirteen. From the summit of Three Rock Mountain I looked across to the gently rolling slopes to the Two Rock summit. A huge fire the previous year had burned the deep heather almost down to the dry, peat-covered bedrock, leaving only blackened stalks that crunched under my feet. Halfway across the slope I spotted a movement in a shallow depression and saw a hare crouching low in the nearly bare ground. I quickly pointed the gun and fired off one barrel, not really trying to aim properly. There was a scream – almost a human cry – and the hare darted off. I had obviously hit it but not fatally. I stood for a second, appalled. The piercing cry continued, all the way to where the animal had disappeared over the skyline and then the distressing sound faded away. At first I had no idea what to do, but after a minute or two I ran after the wounded creature, wondering all the while what I would do if I caught up with it. Would I have the heart to put it out of its misery, or maybe it was not too seriously hurt and the hare had only had a big fright and would have disappeared? Over the skyline there was nothing to be seen, only a vast expanse of unburnt heather and no further sound. I knew, however, that I was responsible for inflicting extreme suffering on an animal that was now dying in misery or was already dead. That was my first and last hunting expedition.

My father had other guns but these were hidden away, or so he thought. A wooden pelmet hid the top of the wardrobe in my parents' bedroom and it was here that they assumed that secrets could be hidden from us children. Little did they know that I at least had long since discovered the Christmas presents from Santa in advance of the great day. It was by accident that I found the guns. I was checking out the concealed presents, without telling my two younger brothers and baby sister, when I reached back and pulled out a cloth bag. It contained two revolvers, a Colt 45 and a Webley. I knew about the Colt since this was a signature weapon in Western cowboy novels. It was much older, being slightly rusty and was obviously a legacy of my father's activities in the War of Independence. The Webley was quite new and was in a leather holster. The Local Defence Force had just been formed at the start of World War II, or the Emergency as it was called in Ireland. My father was chosen as local commander and I was soon to see him proudly don his uniform, complete with Sam Browne belt and Webley sidearm.

I took the Colt one morning when my mother and father were going out and had left me in charge. There was a small leather pouch in the gun bag, which contained six large bullets. I went outside, tried one in the Colt and pulled the trigger. My hand was almost shattered; at least it felt that way. The bullet ricocheted off the stone wall. I was lucky not to be hit by fragments. I carefully replaced the revolver and hoped that my father would not count the bullets. He did buy me a gun for one birthday, however, possibly hoping to convert me into becoming a hunter. It was an air gun and he brought me into the famous gun and fishing gear shop in Parliament Street. I was allowed to pick out my present and I carried it proudly home.

The opportunity to use it was not long in coming. A favourite playground for my brothers and me was a small abandoned quarry hole just above our house. I had made a model sailing boat and we were trying it out in the pond when it occurred to me that it would make a good target for my new weapon. We put the boat into the water with the sail set and the wind took it off, scooting across the water. I took aim and fired just as Eamon stuck out his hand to catch the boat as it drifted into his reach. Unfortunately, I did not see him do this and my pellet round hit him in the hand. It had lodged in the soft tissue between his thumb and first finger, where we could actually see it. I took my penknife and told Eamon that it would be easy to get the pellet out and not to worry. He must have trusted me; after all, I was seventeen months older. I prised the lead pellet out with the tip of the knife and we each agreed that the operation was to remain a secret. Eamon stoically endured the pain and never revealed the truth of the incident. I don't, however, remember what happened to the gun. Maybe my father did find out about my carelessness.

It was the day he shot the goat that has lasted so long in my memory. We were all in the living room one summer evening when my father suddenly shouted, 'Would you look at that bastard goat?'

The window to the living room faced out to the stone wall boundary of the adjoining field. A large nanny goat was standing on top of the wall, calmly munching the leaves of a small tree. My father dashed into his bedroom, emerged with his shotgun, took aim and fired through the open pane. The goat was instantly killed and dropped off the wall. I do remember that my first reaction was that it was a good riddance. We had been plagued by intrusions of goats and the sometimes near destruction of the vegetable plots that my Uncle Jem lovingly attended. On top of that, we had one of those scare campaigns to prevent the invasion of foot and mouth disease from Britain, and allowing animals to stray was strictly forbidden. My father's action was, therefore, within the law, if not particularly orthodox.

My father and I went out and loaded the dead animal into a wheelbarrow. To my surprise, he ordered me to 'take it onto the mountain and bury it'. I accepted the challenge because it seemed to me to be an acknowledgement of my status as the eldest in the family and the one who could carry out this important task. I set out with a gaggle of siblings and other local children who had been attracted by the news of the goat's demise. It was a short wheel to the start of the track onto the mountain, where I had identified a little quarry hole near the road.

Before we tumbled the animal into a small depression, I noticed the goat's full udder. 'Shall we try to milk it first?' I said. The others were highly enthusiastic and someone found a reasonably clean can. The milking was easy and I offered it around the group. The unanimous verdict was that the taste was horrible. One small girl, however, said that what we were doing was a mortal sin but I assured her that it wasn't.

'We were making sure the milk didn't go to waste,' I said. 'That would have been a real mortal sin.' The group accepted this, coming from the acknowledged leader of the enterprise.

'We will have a proper funeral,' I said, and this seemed to satisfy everyone. We carefully piled small stones over the dead animal and then covered it up with grass sods that were lying nearby. Somebody said a short prayer and we made a little cross from dead twigs and then we all, solemnly, said goodbye to 'Mrs. Nanny Goat'.

My father's most affluent times were in the late 1930s. He sometimes bought us expensive presents; I remember the Hornby train sets and the exciting visits to Elvery's sports and toy shop in Dublin. But it was another visit to that gun and fishing shop in Parliament Street that I remember best. My father had been offering to take us fishing and the time had come for each of us to be equipped with proper rods. We had tried hazel sticks and bent pins for hooks in Malone's Pond, without result. Giant trout were rumoured to be lurking there, feeding on the unwanted dogs and cats that were routinely drowned in the pond, I supposed. I think that my father's main motive, however, was to find a recreation that he and his children could enjoy together. We each got a beautiful new fishing rod with reels and line and also packs of mysterious hooks and feathers. Our first outing, I think, was to the Avonmore River where it flows under a stone bridge just below the village of Laragh in County Wicklow. I remember well that first fishing expedition: the brown water of the mountain river swirling over rocks into a deep still pool. None of us hooked anything that day, but it didn't matter. It was fun to spend the day with our father. I can't recall any other fishing trip with him; his enthusiasm simply died away. My father's various enthusiasms were unbounded, his near obsession to start new ventures led to mercurial changes of direction. We never knew what was coming next.

Every time I had to go to Mrs. Mulligan's cottage her Sacred Heart of Jesus transfixed me. It dominated one wall of her kitchen. The little red lamp in front was always lit, but the picture itself just blazed with colour. The head of Jesus stood out from a golden glow but it was the heart that kept me spellbound whenever I stepped into her kitchen: a deep crimson, with a loop of entwined thorns and drops of scarlet blood dripping down. It was the highlight of my day when, as a weekly task, I took our washing down to Mrs. Mulligan.

The journey there and back was on stepping-stones over the little stream that flowed from the mountain to our local washerwoman's little two-roomed cottage. On a dry day, white sheets billowed in the wind, while on calmer days they would be draped across the maze of furze bushes behind the cottage.

There was another little cottage close to Mrs. Mulligan's; we always knew it as Countess Markievicz's cottage. She was one of the leaders in the 1916 Rising and in the aftermath was sentenced to death. The sentence was commuted and she was sent to prison in England. She was eventually released and immediately became deeply involved in the subsequent War of Independence. As a result, she was often on the run from the Black and Tans and the little cottage in the fields below our house was her hiding place. She joined the anti-Treaty side in the Civil War. My father, who was also a supporter of de Valera, the leader of the anti-Treaty side, always held that our area was effectively out of bounds for the British forces. He never spoke of the Civil War.

The cottage remained unused after the Countess's death in 1927 and gradually became semi-ruined, although it would be the site of a few commemorations over the years. Several decades later the well-loved eccentric Eoin ('The Pope') O'Mahony moved into it as a squatter. The Pope, a nickname he acquired when he said that his ambition was to be Pope, was a barrister and genealogist whose eccentricities led him into a somewhat nomadic existence. I met him often on the Slate Cabin Lane where he announced that he was on his way to Malone's Pond for his daily ablutions. He was always cheerful and loquacious and entertained me with his stories. He would travel into the city on the Enniskerry bus and all the passengers would be amused by his various dissertations, delivered in his loud but clear and lovely Cork accent.

The Sandyford Carnegie Library was next door to St Mary's National School. It consisted of one large rectangular room and a couple of small spaces just off the entrance hall. One long wall had open shelves housing mainly romantic novels and a particularly large collection of 'westerns'. The other long wall had a line of separate, enclosed, glass-fronted book cabinets: these were always kept locked. There was a fireplace on the wall beside the open shelves. After my initial visit, the library became my favourite haunt. It was that line of locked, glazed cabinets that seduced me: it seemed like forbidden fruit. It wasn't long after my first visit that I began to establish a regular pattern. This was usually in the early evenings when the open fire would be lit. The librarian might be reading a newspaper by the warm blaze or else playing cards with a few men. He would silently hand me the key to the locked shelves and I would plunge into a glorious treasury of beautifully bound volumes. I remember only two authors: *The Complete Works of Walter Scott* and *The Complete Works of James Fenimore Cooper*. The latter's *The Last of the Mohicans* I could never forget but Walter Scott would likely have bored me to tears.

I did make the occasional foray to the open shelves, and Zane Grey was an immediate antidote to Scott: *Riders of the Purple Sage* and *Lone Star Ranger* had me galloping over high desert country, dreaming of sandstone bluffs, tall cactus and tumbleweed blowing in the wind, all the way back up the Slate Cabin Lane. When I discovered Jack London, I persuaded my father to read *White Fang*. He had never read a book in his life but said he enjoyed the experience. However, I don't think he ever read another.

I never tired of the view from our house on that high road in Woodside, but only a few minutes' climb up the mountain above our garden would lift the horizon to an even more spectacular panorama. The excavation of waste from the old quarry hole that eventually became Malone's Pond was carted to the downward slope and then canted. Many loads built up to form a high flat balcony that over the years became a grassy and significant viewing point, an enticing 'belvedere'. I often sat there to be enveloped by the immense prospect before me. Directly in front, the great bulk of the Howth peninsula formed the outer side of Dublin Bay. I remember the sea as always an intense blue but when the tide went far out on Sandymount Strand, the blue was washed to a pale shade that was almost white. The sands of Bull Island shone yellow in sunshine and I could lament that our house, facing north and under Three Rock Mountain, sat in gloomy shadow while the wide curve of Dublin Bay would be in sunlit splendour. On a clear day I could see the blue grey peaks of the Mourne Mountains on the northern horizon, with the pyramid of the solitary Slieve Gullion marking the frontier of north and south. It was far more exciting, however, on a calm frosty morning, to gaze to the east and suddenly there was Snowdon. The Irish Sea was no longer an ocean and Wales seemed just a stone's throw away. I always felt that the 'belvedere' was my eyrie.

Only a few days after my brother Eamon and I arrived, for the first time, at Synge Street Christian Brothers School, one of the Brothers said, 'Ah, here come the mountainy men'. Synge Street CBS was essentially an urban school in those days, the majority of the pupils being city boys. It was 1938 and the city of Dublin was more contained. The suburbs beyond the canals effectively still had villages or townships, like Ballsbridge, Rathmines and Rathgar, while farther out we had Rathfarnam, Windy Arbour and Dundrum. Sandyford, Stepaside and particularly Barnacullia were exotic country places where city dwellers could go for holidays. The field beside our house had three small wooden huts where people would come from Dublin to stay in the summer.

It was a long journey to school: a three-mile cycle to Dundrum and then the train to the terminus at Harcourt Street.

It meant an early start to each day. The ride to Dundrum was nearly downhill all the way but the uphill slog to home at the end of each afternoon was long and tedious, invariably with homework still to be faced.

I was a lonely small boy for those first few months in Synge Street. Eamon was placed two classes lower than me, and we rarely met in school-time. The city was an alien place to me after the open fields, the great sweep of heather hillside and the huge wild playground of quarry holes on Three Rock Mountain, as well as the dens, carefully cut into the dense hedgerows of Woodside. After a while, however, I came to realise that the city could have new and very different attractions.

One of the first was Craddock's shop on Harrington Street, to be passed each day on the way to school. My collecting bug had expanded from pressing wildflowers to stamp-collecting, and Craddock's had window displays of extreme seduction. The Bumper Assortment of 1000 was the highlight but the sets from exotic places like Bhutan, Tahiti, Hong Kong, Mongolia, St Helena, Papua, Borneo and Easter Island were to be greatly desired. The stamps from these far-off places were often quite large and colourful, featuring strange animals, birds and flora. I never felt any attraction to the esoteric desire to acquire specimens such as Penny Blacks or other rare items. I thought that such obsessions were boring and, anyway, I could never afford them. I lusted, however, for the sumptuous stamp albums, often with beautifully embossed hard covers and stiff pages, each with lines of transparent slots for the displays of treasures. I, sadly, had to make do with cheap paper albums, where each newly found treasure had to be fixed with annoyingly sticky mounts.

The other great urban attraction was the discovery of the little shops selling second-hand comics. My pocket money hardly extended beyond one new comic a week, but here was a treasure trove of countless old editions of the *Rover*, *Hotspur* and *Champion* and all for a few pence. My city explorations during lunchtime stretched down Charlemont Street and along the length of Camden Street. There was one old second-hand bookshop at the bottom of Camden Street which sold used schoolbooks, so we had a legitimate reason for going down there. Capaldi's ice cream shop, with the little wooden booths inside, was also a Mecca for delicious treats. Most boys could go home for lunch each day but that was not possible for the pupils from the country. My explorations for the first months in my new school were solitary ones, which reinforced the loneliness I experienced in that unhappy period. Soon, however, I acquired my first friends at school and began to fit into the new reality of being part of this huge and boisterous community. I learned to live with the continual uproar of hundreds of small boys and the distress of the frequent loud punishments that echoed around the confines of that concrete yard.

It was always called the 'yard', not the schoolyard, and certainly never the playground. It was a concrete-floored rectangle, with one-half shaded by the tall school buildings. Lower brick walls enclosed the other half that, facing north, got little sunshine. For me, coming from the playground at St Mary's, with the sycamore trees and green fields all around and open to the sun, it was an intimidating place. I had hardly been at the school more than a few weeks when, during one lunchtime, the yard filled with hundreds of juniors; I heard a growing yelling. At one end of the yard a crowd began a rush up the centre chasing one small boy, who eventually escaped up the narrow steel fire escape to the upper classrooms. The mob swarmed around the base of the stairs chanting 'Monkey O'Dea, Monkey O'Dea, Monkey O'Dea', while the terrified boy crouched halfway up the steps staring down at his tormentors. I had made no friends at that stage to ask what was going on and, anyway, it seemed safer to stay away from trouble. It may have been the boy's appearance that sparked the taunting. Only in later years, whenever I remembered that incident, did Down's Syndrome come to mind. I thought of Blacky, the loner, who was also something of an outcast and I kept well to the outskirts of the crowd until the bell for classes ended the affair. This happened again and again over the next few weeks until the mob got tired of the bullying but, for me, it was a hard beginning to my new urban schooldays.

The yard was also used for gym classes. These were neither imaginative nor pleasurable, consisting of a short session of bending, stretching and jumping, all the boys lined up in rigid lines and squares, followed by a longer session of 'route marches'. These were favourites of the newly formed Local Defence Force in the early days of World War II. The gym teacher was a retired army man, short, stout and with little understanding of the schoolboy world. His outdoor classes were unpopular, particularly the boring marching. He would stand and shout through a tin loudhailer. We soon found that a simple way of annoying him, sometimes to the extent of rage, was the CRASH, two, three, four. A hundred or more leather soles pounding the concrete on the first step of four. This had a most satisfying loud echo from the surrounding walls. You had to be careful not to let him see you do it because he usually stood in the centre of the yard. He sometimes got so enraged that he would hit the nearest boy on the head with his tin megaphone. When the class ended, there were whoops of triumph in the rush back to our schoolrooms.

The yard did, however, become a place of shame and punishment for me quite early on. The train from Dundrum to

Harcourt Street was often slow-moving and could stop for a brief period on the bridge over the Grand Canal before entering the station terminus. One morning on the way to school, I was sharing a compartment with two other Synge Street boys, each of us ten years old and from the same class. When the train stopped just before entering the station, we discovered that our compartment was directly over the canal. We lowered the window to get a good view and quickly decided to have a competition to see who could spit into the water. When we tired of this fun, we turned to find that a lone man who was sharing the compartment with us was examining some of our copybooks, having opened our school bags. We, naively at first, thought that he was interested in our schoolwork and talked jokingly with him. He said nothing but just smiled at us as the train jolted to a start. We then had to rush from the station to avoid being late for class, not knowing that he was a teacher in the secondary school.

That same morning in class there was a rude awakening for us after only an hour or so of lessons. A messenger arrived and there was a whispered conversation with our teacher, who then looked up and called out our three names. We were ordered to stand up and go the office of the school principal to explain our behaviour on the train that morning. The principal told us that we were a disgrace to the school and would be punished. He ordered us to stand in the centre of the yard during break-time, when the other junior classes would witness our beating. He also said that it would be a warning to others to always behave properly outside school hours. It was a miserable time waiting for the break but when it came we three took up our position in the centre of the yard while the other classes stood around, keeping a respectable distance from the condemned.

I had just read, in one of my comics, the story of Captain Dreyfus, the French army officer who was falsely accused in 1894 of delivering defence secrets to the Germans, and the way he was publicly humiliated and disgraced. We, however, were undoubtedly guilty and deserved what was coming to us. While awaiting my turn – I was last – I imagined myself as the gallant Captain, having his decorations and epaulettes torn off and the final debasement of seeing his sword broken in two. I don't remember if it helped much because I received the three hard slaps, on each hand, from the dreaded black leather. The Brother who often administered punishments was, naturally, an unpopular figure. His nickname was The Snots. He did his task with vigour and enthusiasm, always with a smiling face. Somehow the whole episode was not too much of a disgrace, in the eyes of our peers at least. It was impossible to be detached while forced to watch another pupil being beaten, often savagely. There was a sense of relief, certainly, of not being the recipient of the chastisement, but more often there was, instead, a strong feeling of fellowship with the victim of the punishment. After all, 'they' were the enemy, in what could be a daily war, as the sounds of violence echoed around that yard.

I did acquire a couple of friends in the first few months at Synge Street. There was a boy called Larry DeJong, who was also one of the small number of pupils from outside the city. I remember him telling me me that his parents had moved from Holland to north Dublin where they had established a vegetable farm. I have forgotten the name of the other boy, who was from the very centre of the city: his home was in an old Georgian house on Wood Quay. I have a distinct memory of a visit there and of that terrace of tall, gaunt old buildings, facing out to the dark waters of the Liffey. He was a staunch friend to me in that unsettling time, always good-humoured, positive and unafraid of the sometimes brutal regime. His ambition was to be a fireman. He certainly helped me to cope with the daily stress in that big city school.

For my second year in Synge Street I was placed in a classroom presided over by two lay teachers. One we always called Mr. Doherty, the other was Francis MacManus. We all knew that he was a famous writer and that a new novel of his had just been published: the title was *Men Withering*. I was in Mr. Doherty's class but sometimes the two teachers swopped places. I remember that Mr. MacManus was quite a jolly character and even though punishments were a daily feature of lessons and were rarely good-humoured, there was one incident where he had both classes laughing. A boy was to be punished for giving a wrong answer in a religious class and Mr. MacManus ordered him to bend over a chair so that he could be beaten on the bottom. After the first smack of the leather, MacManus stopped and ordered the unfortunate victim to remove the object that he, the boy, had stuffed down his trousers. Sheepishly, an open schoolbook was handed over and Mr. MacManus cheerfully announced to the whole room, 'Look what we have here – the Catechism, an appropriate defence against his religious ignorance'. The room erupted with the released tension, the sentence was repealed and class resumed in high good humour.

I was not so lucky some time later. Homework copybooks had to be handed up each morning and when Mr. Doherty opened mine, he ordered me to stand out to the front of the class. 'Your handwriting is a disgrace,' he said and then quoted the old Irish proverb, '*Cad a scríobhan an púca, tuig leis féin é a léamh*', translated as 'What the puca writes, he can read himself.' 'This merits six of the best', Mr Doherty said and produced the leather to give me three hard blows on each hand.

Back at my desk, I held my burning palms around the cold, cast iron legs of the desk and just about held back the tears at the injustice of the punishment. I always wrote too fast, because ideas flowed, but this inevitably could look like carelessness. The content of the homework, an essay perhaps, did not seem to matter to the teacher, only its appearance. It seemed to me particularly unjust because I had got top marks for my essay only a few days previously. I think that the title of the essay was 'A Day in the Life of a Shilling'.

Wednesday afternoon was set aside for sports, attendance at which was compulsory. The sports ground was a considerable distance away from Synge Street and for me a lot farther from the railway station. A much later and longer journey home was not, however, the only, or even the main, problem for me. I just hated team sports and the only activity offered was Gaelic football. This seemed to consist of a crowd of schoolboys rushing around in a confused mass, pushing, screaming, taunting and kicking while the sports master shouted a tirade of orders, reproofs and sarcasm from the touchline.

The only alternative available was to join the art class. This was to be my sanctuary during those early, unhappy months at Synge Street Christian Brothers School. I have the fondest memories of Brother Arnold, the art teacher, a kindly and jovial soul who managed to make school a satisfying and pleasurable experience, at least for that one afternoon of the week. The classes were not held in the main school but in a small house in Heytesbury Street, at the rear of the school. Brother Arnold informed us newcomers vehemently that his 'Art Academy' had no connection whatever with that adjoining institution, CBS Synge Street. We delighted in that feeling of being special and embraced with enthusiasm the illusion that we young artists were entirely divorced from the oppressive regime next door. Although Brother Arnold did introduce us to unfamiliar techniques – woodblock and linocut printing, for instance – it was the sheer freedom of experimentation he allowed that opened a creativity far removed from my early tussles, in St Mary's, with the 'cursèd teapot'.

I continued to attend Brother Arnold's 'Academy' each Wednesday afternoon for seven years. It was the foundation for my life in art and particularly in drawing, and his name and inspirational enthusiasm lives long in my memory.

My move from the last year in the primary school into the secondary must have been seamless. I remember little of my early years there except that I managed to avoid being in the class presided over by the teacher who was responsible for reporting me for the canal-spitting incident. The secondary school was housed in the two-storey houses that lined one side of the lower section of Synge Street. This gave a cosy and in-timate atmosphere to the classes, which were housed in sepa-rate sections. At this stage I had found two friends, Bernard and Aidan, and we three went on to become firm companions for all my remaining years in Synge Street and for many years later. I no longer felt alone in what had once been an alien place, and school life and young life could be embraced with fun, and increasingly with gusto.

Opera became a new enthusiasm and we three, as we often described ourselves, eagerly awaited the opera season in the Gaiety Theatre. We could only afford the 'Gods', the highest balcony with hard wooden benches. The tickets, however, were cheap: I seem to remember sixpence. Our very first experience and one that is firmly fixed in my memory was a performance of *Pagliacci* and *Cavalleria Rusticana*, short operas usually coupled in the one evening. The chorus for the Gaiety season usually came from the Rathmines and Rathgar

Musical Society, all amateurs. A cynic observed that for one opera – it might have been *Aida* – you could see the marks of sock suspenders on the legs of some of the toga wearers. In those days suspenders were essential to hold up one's socks.

Midway during my time in secondary school was the year with 'The Guck'. This was Brother Lucy, one of the most unpopular teachers in Synge Street. He was tall and thin with a cadaverous face; I never remember him smiling. He knew about his nickname, as I'm sure most teachers were aware of their own. 'That's a terrible name to call a holy man,' he would say, often when handing out punishments. He had very large feet and would sometimes say, 'Come closer, boy' and then stamp on the boy's toes. He had a pocket in his long, often dusty, black soutane, where he stowed his leather strap, ready for use. We did not take long to discover that he also kept there a small bottle of whiskey, a 'Baby Power'. His famous ruse was to start his 'lending library' as a way to support his tipple. This was a collection of dog-eared books that could be borrowed for a few pennies. I seem to remember that he stated that it was compulsory to join his library. Some of the books were religious, but I have no memory of any of the titles. We hated the whole nature of the scheme.

It was only many decades later that I softened my memory of The Guck and felt some sympathy. He was, after all, a lonely elderly man who, as a Christian Brother, had none of the status that an ordained priest enjoyed. He had little money and a long and celibate life was to be his lot.

My last two years in Synge Street were the best years of my school life. I no longer felt either alone or an outsider. I was by now well settled into that crowded, sometimes almost hostile, community. More than anything, however, was the influence of one teacher who changed my life and made every day in his class a joy and an inspiration. His name was Tommy O'Rourke. We did have Brother Creed also in those final years and I remember him as friendly and good-humoured. Tommy was our English teacher. He may have taught other subjects, but the pleasure of his English class erased any memory of these. It is interesting that I even remember where he lived, even though I didn't pass it on the way to school. His house was on Dundrum Road, directly opposite the great granite wall of what was then called the Lunatic Asylum, now the Central Mental Hospital.

Tommy O'Rourke's love of poetry was paramount and this love was easily passed on to those of us who were open to it as a gift for a lifetime. He was grounded in the classics, Keats and Shelley in particular, but also Milton and Tennyson. Shakespeare's Sonnets were often quoted and I have embedded in my memory 'Bare ruin'd choirs, where late the sweet birds sang', and who could find anything more romantic than:

> Shall I compare thee to a summer's day?
> Thou art more lovely and more temperate:
> Rough winds do shake the darling buds of May,
> And summer's lease hath all too short a date:

I don't remember any major reference to modern poets. It was the 1940s, after all, but it must have been in Tommy's class that the poetry of Gerard Manley Hopkins was introduced to us. I well remember our teacher's enthusiastic praise of Hopkins's use of alliteration and above all onomatopoeia in his work. It was not surprising that Synge Street School accepted this modernistic poet. Hopkins was a Jesuit and the school was firmly Roman Catholic, as well as Republican, at that time. However, I don't remember that the religious element of the poems featuring in any discussions. It was always about the richness of language and the beauty of the nature poems. I loved an early poem, 'Pied Beauty':

Glory be to God for dappled things –
 For skies of couple-colour as a brinded cow;
  For rose-moles all in stipple upon trout that swim;
Fresh-firecoal chestnut-falls; finches' wings;
 Landscape plotted and pieced – fold, fallow, and plough;
  And all trades, their gear and tackle and trim.

Tommy O'Rourke's favourite Irish poet was Francis Ledwidge and his unbridled love of the poems was transmitted to me as a schoolboy. I still have my copy of *The Collected Poems of Francis Ledwidge,* published in London by Herbert Jenkins, and lines from the works often swim through my thoughts. Tommy's choice poem was 'Lament for Thomas MacDonagh':

He shall not hear the bittern cry
In the wild sky, where he is lain,
Nor voices of the sweeter birds
Above the wailing of the rain.

There was a photograph of Francis Ledwidge in an initial page of the book. It showed a young man, solemn-faced, dressed in a cumbersome-looking military greatcoat. His hair was dark, as was his then fashionable moustache. His lament for Thomas MacDonagh was that he would never again 'hear the bittern cry in the wild sky' and this could be his own epitaph. He would die in the mud and blood of the Great War.

My own selections have been in the early poems such as 'June' but 'A Twilight in Middle March' always delights:

Within the oak a throb of pigeon wings
Fell silent, and grey twilight hushed the fold,
And spiders' hammocks swung on half-oped things
That shook like foreigners upon our cold.
A gipsy lit a fire and made a sound
Of moving tins, and from an oblong moon
The river seemed to gush across the ground
To the cracked metre of a marching tune.

We had two Shakespeare plays for those final school years, *Julius Caesar* and, in the last year, *Hamlet*. Our English teacher's guidance through these works was always enjoyable and inspiring. I remember that Tommy O'Rourke once said that Shakespeare was often sanitised for school editions and that unexpurgated Shakespeare should be the norm. The study of *Hamlet* was so engaging that I still have a visual memory of the story, helped no doubt by the beautiful black and white film of 1948, with the magisterial Laurence Olivier as the tragic hero. In Brother Arnold's Art class that year he produced for us a reproduction of the Millais painting *Ophelia*. That image of Ophelia just floating in her long dress in the dark water, under a bower of green willows, white flowers and reeds, would stay long in my memory.

It could be no coincidence or surprise that many notable personalities in the Irish arts world went to Synge Street and that their English teacher was Tommy O'Rourke. Pearse Hutchinson was one year ahead of my final class and he published a short piece for the school yearbook which praised the Neo-Gothic St Kevin's Church next door to the school. He was, however, a hero to us in sixth year more for his slightly rebel reputation than for his status as a putative poet.

Our own class of 1945/46 had its share of personalities who would shine in the years after school. Richard Power was the quiet one: I remember him at his desk at the back of the class. We knew that he was beginning his writings, mostly in Irish at that time. We also heard that he had a small wooden shed at the bottom of his garden where he would retire to work. Richard went on to write his novel *The Hungry Grass*, which deals with the essential loneliness of the priesthood. I still have my copy, for a long time out of print, but now, desirably, republished in a new edition. I sometimes wonder if the writer in Richard saw the same loneliness in the Christian Brothers who taught us at Synge Street. Richard died young, one year after his novel was published in 1969. Anthony Hughes was also in my class. Music was his forte, although we had no music teaching at the school. He went on to further studies and eventually became Professor of Music at University College Dublin. It was sad when I met Anthony after he retired. He told me that, because of health problems, he could no longer play the piano.

Patrick Swift shared a desk with me for that final year; we all called him Paddy at the time. He was an extraordinary young man: he had an intellect well beyond his years and was an insatiable reader of books. Paddy was also an accomplished artist, even in those early years. He introduced me to James Joyce and most of all to *Ulysses*; we were just seventeen. This was at a period when the mass banning of books raged through Catholic Ireland. On top of our own Irish campaign against 'evil literature', there was the Index of condemned books, promulgated by the Vatican. Strangely *Ulysses* was never banned in Ireland. I distinctly remember seeing a copy of the book in a Dublin bookshop. It was on a high shelf where a ladder or the help of an assistant was needed to reach it. I was far too timid to ask for the notorious work; I could never have afforded it anyway. I have no idea where or how Paddy got his copy. I also risked excommunication by reading Gustave Flaubert's *Madame Bovary*, in translation of course.

There was one incident in Tommy's English class that stands out. Our homework was an essay. I can't remember the subject we were given but some of us were called out to read to the group. It was Paddy's turn and Tommy asked him to stand out in front of the class for his reading. Tommy sat impassively as Paddy began. It was a flowing presentation for about ten minutes, but when Paddy began to quote the poetry of Baudelaire, he started to falter a little. After a pause Tommy said, 'That was good, Paddy, very good considering you have written only three lines.' The class exploded – we all knew that Paddy had written very little. Tommy smiled. I don't think there was any retribution, only that he had to actually write the essay.

When Paddy Swift and I left school we met briefly at night classes in the National College of Art. After those classes, I never met Paddy again. He had a colourful career, moving first to London, where he founded and edited, after the 1940s, the literary magazine *X*, a quarterly review of art and literature. He had a solo exhibition of his paintings in the Waddington Gallery, Dublin in 1952 which was widely praised. I loved his tree paintings, but found his other work gloomy. In 1962 he moved to Portugal where he briefly dabbled in ceramics. He finally settled in the Algarve where he painted and wrote but sadly died at the early age of fifty-six. I have always regretted that I never really got to know him well as we both moved into separate careers, but he had a major influence on me when we were schoolboys together in Synge Street.

My arrival on a motorbike for the start of the school year in September 1945 caused a sensation. The war in Europe had ended in May and shortly afterwards the Irish army sold off much of its wartime equipment. My father bought me an ex-army motorbike: it was a BSA, M20 side valve model, 500cc, painted military green, and I loved it. It was far too big and too powerful for me, a lightweight who struggled to lift it onto its stand. Still, I soon got the knack, and the sheer pleasure of roaring into that concrete schoolyard was worth every effort. Brother Creed met me on that first morning and it was good to see the smile on his face. He said that the machine was 'a cross between a racing car and a tractor' and then helped me to wheel it into the Brothers' quarters; it would have been too much of a temptation to the other boys. On my way home, a crowd would gather around to watch my departure. I was now expert at kick-starting the machine and it was a satisfying blast of noise, echoing off the school walls, as I rode out of the gate. I felt that I had finally triumphed over the yard that had so intimidated me as an eleven-year-old from rural County Dublin. It was useful for me to have access to my father's garage. I had little money, so servicing and fills of petrol were free.

I loved the freedom that machine gave me. In just ten minutes I could speed up to the Pine Forest, and then, on an almost traffic-free road, race over the Featherbed and up the steep hill towards the lonely Sally Gap. Sometimes in summer I could park the bike and scramble down to Upper Lough Bray, and swim in the dark amber water. Later, when I became more skilful in managing that monster of a machine, I ventured to tackle the Military Road from the Sally Gap to Glendalough. In the early post-war years this was merely a rough track, sand-surfaced and winding sinuously across the immense moorland of the Wicklow Mountains. I often had to pause for a rest and let the engine cool, but most of all I wanted to savour the solitude. This may have been the beginning, I realised later, of my need to seek out a wild place: a challenge or adventure, perhaps, or maybe most of all the sheer pleasure of being totally alone.

High up, a mossy clearing in the Pine Forest was a perfect refuge to sunbathe, and to swot for the coming June exams, but one day the road past the woods towards Glencullen very nearly ended my solitary expeditions. In 1947 there were exceptional snowfalls, with immense drifts that made the upper mountain roads impassable. The snow filled the ditches beside the roads, and had hardly melted well into the month of May. The roads also became potholed after the thaw. On one of those early summer days, a day of balmy air and long lingering sunshine, the bike smashed into a deep hole and, still attached by one leg to the sprawling bike, I careered along the road, until a grass bank ended the slide.

One handlebar was snapped off, the petrol tank had a huge dent, and the front wheel was badly damaged. When I managed to stand upright, I could feel severe pain down my left side and past my hip. The fact that I was wearing several pairs of trousers probably saved me from a more serious injury, but I knew that I was badly gashed. My left arm had only small scrapes because it was protected by my heavy leather jacket. I had to sit on the bank for almost an hour before a car stopped and the driver took me home. At the time I felt that this episode could spell the end of my motorcycling days, and my freedom to roam wherever I wished. This was in fact the most serious of several minor spills I had over the first few months of tearing around in such joyous ecstasy. My mother was always worried that one day I might be taken home, if not dead, at least crippled for life. She never approved of my father buying the bike for me. I decided before I reached home that I would not tell her about the great gash in my side. The several pairs of trousers had managed to soak up and partially disguise the blood that had earlier flowed freely. I locked myself in the bathroom, washed off the blood and stuck plasters over the gash.

I had the freshly repaired machine back in a couple of weeks. I boasted, years later, that my motorcycling days made me a better driver. 'You were just bloody lucky,' a good friend said. 'You could just as easily be dead.'

There was one boy who was often late for after-lunch classes. He would usually try to sneak in, hoping not to be noticed, but he was always spotted and invariably punished. One afternoon the classroom door burst open and in the boy rushed, shouting, 'War has been declared.'

It was 3 September 1939 and the start of what became World War II or The Emergency. At first there was little change in our daily lives at school or at home. However, even though Ireland was neutral, the fear of gas attacks meant that gas masks were issued. As it transpired, only city-dwellers qualified for this precaution, so school-goers from outside the city were excluded. I don't remember that this exclusion caused me the least concern at the time; the war would change utterly our predictable daily routine and offer new and exciting possibilities. These were certainly the thoughts of a twelve-year-old schoolboy: our parents would have different thoughts and concerns.

At home, my father's time had come. The threat of a possible invasion led to the setting up of the Local Defence Force or the LDF, as it became universally known. This was to be a reserve army of part-time soldiers, thus boosting Ireland's puny regular force. It must have been my father's service in the War of Independence that earned him command of the local battalions of that force, and he entered the role with enthusiasm. He could be a natural leader, and his entrepreneurial exploits, although some were failures, at least spoke of imagination and great enthusiasm. At first the bands of eager recruits had neither uniforms nor weapons, as an early photograph of a grand parade of the newly formed force in Stepaside showed. My father is on a makeshift-reviewing stand – the back of an open lorry – alongside the local garda sergeant, while the motley parade marches past. Belted overcoats, raincoats, old clothes and best suits, complete with hats and caps, were the norm. There were a few guns, shotguns mainly, and one tall man carries a make-believe machine gun, fashioned from a length of pipe.

The uniforms and weapons eventually arrived and the route marches were now impressively military. The rhythmic clash of hundreds of hobnailed boots on tarmac was a novel and exciting sound to us schoolboys, as we followed the troops on our bicycles. Those early days of the Emergency saw a new spirit of community, with the organisation of fund-raising, such as whist drives and dances. A contemporary photograph, taken at the dance hall in The Scalp, shows a large gathering of uniformed LDF posing, while behind are massed the wives and girlfriends, smiling at the camera. My father, along with a few other officers, is at the front, while my mother, looking happy, is in one of the rows behind.

For me, the outbreak of the war opened up the prospect of a heady mixture of adventure, excitement and even drama. Wartime literature, magazines and boys' comics showed illustrations that helped to identify all types of military aircraft. These were now to be seen and heard with increasing frequency over the east coast of Ireland. There were also scare stories of possible hostile happenings, reported as warnings but then inflated as rumours. One such in the early months of the war was of the danger of parachutists dropping in for some nefarious purpose: spying was one suggestion. Woodside and Barnacullia were galvanised one morning with the rumour that a parachutist had been spotted landing near the top of Three Rock Mountain. I rushed out and ran up the path beside my grandmother's house to get a better look, and there on the sky-line was a definite fluttering of something. I decided to walk up the slope to investigate and then I heard distant gunfire. This stopped me in my tracks, but when silence fell I had to walk on to satisfy my curiosity. The fluttering turned out to be a red flag, with a regular Irish army soldier standing guard holding a rifle and fixed bayonet. He was a sour-faced individual and was obviously bored with his duty. Standing alone on an open hillside for hours did not improve his temper. He told me to clear off and said there was a new Army shooting range in the valley below, now out-of-bounds. It didn't occur to me, on my way down the mountain, to think what I would have done if it had actually been a parachutist.

Real excitement, however, was to come. One early summer morning in 1941 I was on my way from Harcourt Street Station to school. At the top of Camden Street I joined a stream of Synge Street boys coming from various directions when we heard the most tremendous roar of engines. A black fighter bomber with a German cross clearly visible raced above the street at nearly chimneypot level. Two Spitfires were close behind, one just to the rear of the Luftwaffe plane, the other out to the right. The aircraft were gone in a flash, vanishing to the south, as the crowd of schoolboys cheered and waved. Huge arguments ensued: was there definite firing just above our heads? Was the Luftwaffe plane an Me 110 or a Heinkel? Were the RAF planes Spitfires or Hurricanes? We were all experts, or so we thought, at identifying wartime aircraft and so the disputes continued and, as a result, we were all late for classes. We were duly told off but the whole school buzzed for the rest of the day.

Long after the war ended, there was a report that a Luftwaffe Heinkel had been shot down near Carnsore Point in County Wexford and that a RAF Hurricane had been the victor, but had crash-landed nearby later. So we were all correct, at least in some of the sightings.

At about the same time, the summer of 1941, there was a report one morning of a crash landing near my home. We were told that it had just happened in a field off the Ballyogan Road, not far down from Woodside. This was highly exciting news, not least because of the prospect of snapping up souvenirs from the downed plane. I hopped on my bike and, joining a few other local boys, went as fast as possible, hoping to get to the crash site first and claim our treasures. When we arrived at an open gate into a big field, a warplane was sitting there as if parked and not alone perfectly undamaged but well guarded by armed soldiers. We were not allowed to go near it and a sergeant ordered us to go home. I was bitterly disappointed but at least was proud to be able to identify the aircraft as a RAF Bristol Beaufighter. The rumour mill already had a story that the crew were glad to get to a neutral country. After the war, when the facts of wartime crashes and landings were collated, the true story was that the three-man crew had lost their way in bad weather and had almost run out of fuel. The crew was interned, albeit for only a short time, and the plane was purchased for the Irish Air Corps from the British authorities.

I saw the sharp and awful reality of war when there was a bombing of Dublin in May 1941. My father brought me into the city the morning after a German raid. The North Strand suffered the worst damage and I saw the huge crater in the roadway and the devastation caused to so many houses. I was told that there were 28 deaths and scores of people injured: my romantic notions about the adventure of war quickly diminished.

In those early days of the war we had our own dark news when our baby sister Isobel was diagnosed with diphtheria. This was a highly infectious disease and she was instantly removed to the Cork Street Fever Hospital. She spent almost six months there, and the same length of time in the Beneavin Nursing Home in Dublin. I have only blurred memories of those months when she was taken away from 'Woodside'. I do, however, remember the worried faces of our parents as they scanned the evening papers to check that Isobel's number was still there, in the long lists of recovering patients. They were allowed no visitors for the entire time they spent either as patients or as convalescents. The fact that they were each given a number, rather than being named, was presumably for the purpose of anonymity. Isobel was six years old when the ambulance arrived to take her from us, and I remember the joy and relief when she was finally restored to the family.

I still devoured stories about the war and avidly followed the progress of the conflict in the maps of campaigns in the newspapers and magazines. I was fascinated by aircraft and had fantasies of flying a fighter plane. I had been making models of ships, notably an intricate one of the famous clipper ship *The Cutty Sark*. This was now abandoned for a model Spitfire, lovingly painted in camouflage colours and hung from the ceiling of the shed.

Despite Ireland's neutrality, the war did make its mark in many ways. For us schoolboys, the building of massive ugly concrete air raid shelters down the centre of Camden Street was an immediate and brutal reminder to us on our way to school that our world had changed. There was soon a severe shortage of petrol, and cars began to vanish from the streets. My father, in his usual enthusiastic embrace of innovation, bought us a pony. A smart two-wheeled trap also appeared one morning and we now had a new form of transport. The pony's name was Bobby and he had a nasty side to his nature. As the eldest, it was my job to look after him. One of my regular tasks was to take him to the blacksmith's in Stepaside for horseshoeing. I would first have to catch him in the field we had rented, always a long and frustrating job. I then had to ride bareback or else drag an unwilling Bobby all the way to the forge. When I managed to jump up on his back, I had to quickly pull one leg up horizontally to avoid the animal trying to crush it against the roadside stone wall.

When we arrived at the forge, there was usually more trouble. The blacksmith had a bad temper and if Bobby didn't stand still, he would hit him with his hammer on the soft side of his rump. The pony would roll his yellow eyes and I would have to move fast to get out of the way. I became quite expert, however, at harnessing Bobby to the trap and always enjoyed training him to trot along sedately, although he sometimes wanted to gallop, and then we could be nearly unseated. I think it was my father's role in the LDF that enabled him to have his car back, at least for limited journeys. Bobby had to go and I wasn't sorry.

The most severe shortage the war brought was fuel for heating. Almost all our coal was imported and, with the heavy sinking of ships in the Irish Sea and in the Atlantic, there was a near crisis, not just for householders, but for hospitals, schools, offices and every other large building where boilers were invariably fuelled by coal. Dense, choking smog was often the inevitable result of this dependence, but coal was cheap and easily imported from Britain. The answer came with a huge nationwide exploitation of our one great natural resource: our peat bogs.

My father's entrepreneurial skills then came to the fore once more. He rented a large section of bogland near the top of the ridge above Glencullen that formed the boundary between County Dublin and County Wicklow. He then signed a contract with Dublin County Council to supply turf to fuel the boilers of all the hospitals of the county. Six of his lorries were fitted with high-slatted timber sides and it was easy to recruit a large body of men to start the operation. There was already an unpaved roadway down from Boranaraltry Bridge that contoured easily up to an old hunting lodge, which was surrounded by a small coppice of pine trees. There had been an early twentieth-century granite stone quarry nearby but it had been long abandoned. In local memory, the quarry was called 'The Klondike', presumably because it was the source of badly needed employment. This new enterprise was enthusiastically welcomed in the area.

Once the turf banks were opened and the first of millions of sods were cut and laid out to dry, everything seemed to go smoothly. Drying conditions that early summer were normal and after a few weeks the sods were lifted up into 'footings'. There were thousands of these little turf pyramids on the heather-covered strips of bog that separated the lines of cut-tings. Further drying could continue when the footings were heaped up into small loose cairns to complete the process.

Then there was a big question. It was easy enough in a small operation to carry the dried sods in a sack, for instance, to where the load could be collected for transport, but this was now a totally different enterprise. The harvested fuel could be spread over a vast area, and how to carry it easily and efficiently over greater distances to the roadhead was a problem. The first solution was to have a large number of wooden wheelbarrows delivered to the new bogland operation. These were not needed for use until the first dried crop was ready for collection. Then, when that time came, there was consternation. When the barrows were loaded, the wheels sank into the soft surface of the heather-covered access strips between the cuttings and were almost useless. Unfortunately, this early operation was just after a week or so of heavy rain which made the bog surfaces even softer than usual.

The answer came quickly. Generations of turf-cutters in the West of Ireland used donkeys. These animals were equipped with creels – willow woven baskets – on each side, and the donkeys were known to be sure-footed even in the softest conditions. Donkeys were not difficult to find and one morning four splendid specimens arrived in Uncle Mick's part of the field, next door to our house. Three of the animals were jennies (mares) and the fourth was a jack. One was almost jet-black, had floppy ears and immediately became my favourite. I think I was influenced by a story from Irish class called *Mo Asal beag dubh,* 'My Little Black Donkey'. All four were strong-looking, well-fed and, unlike Bobby, docile and even friendly. They were quickly transported up to Glencullen and installed in a field beside Boranaraltry Bridge. I was given a summer job on the bog, specifically to be in charge of the donkeys.

There was an unspoken hierarchy on the bog. At the top were the turf-cutters: skilled experts at use of the *sleán,* a sharp-angled spade, also called a slane in English. These men were valued for their speed and accuracy at slicing a perfect sod and tossing it neatly and unbroken to the top of the bank. Footing was easy, because it could be quickly mastered, just turning the sods upright into a small pinnacle to dry out. There was, however, a special skill that developed with this new large-scale exploitation of the peat resource. When streams of dried sods were brought to the roadhead to await loading on to lorries, it was necessary to make stacks, which could become quite large. It was essential that these stacks were firmly built, stable and, above all, resistant to heavy rainfall. Skilled builders soon emerged from the workforce, particularly a couple of local men from Glencullen. Each sod had to be tilted slightly upwards, to throw off the rain, and an ancient technique, dating back to megalithic stone tomb-builders, was used to form turf stacks. This had been an unbroken tradition in the western boglands for generations but the stacks were now quite enormous. The Glencullen men began to fashion the great stacks into wonderful turf sculptures. The normally straight faces would be formed with a rippled effect of sinuous curves, while the vulnerable extremities would be protected from collapse by beautifully rounded ends. The sculptures did not last long, however, some for maybe just a few hours. When the lorries arrived, all hands were mobilised for a swift loading. The stack would vanish, as a dense rain of sods filled the high slatted body of the lorry and off it would go, grinding in low gear down the rough road and on to the lowlands.

My job was special, I smugly thought. Each morning I would be picked up at my gate and hauled up into a lorry, already partly filled with men. At Boranaraltry Bridge I was dropped off and then had to catch the donkeys and lead them up the hill to the workings. I discovered that I could cut short the journey by heading straight up by the banks of a small stream that drained down from the upper part of the mountain. The donkeys were no trouble and I led them by zigzagging easily up the steeper slopes. The creels were kept in a small wooden hut at the workings and when the donkeys were fitted out, the work of transporting the dried sods could begin. There were a few other boys who were given the job of loading the creels and leading the animals to the roadhead. The donkeys were strong and nimble in their progress, even heavily loaded, down to the large stacks. In the evening, and somewhat earlier than the quitting time for the rest of the workforce, I would take my string of patient four-legged workers back down the mountain to the lush grass in their field. I would wait for my homeward transport at the bridge. I remember well the quiet pleasure of sitting on the stone parapet over the Glencullen River, pleasurably tired after a good day's labour.

The camaraderie in the workforce each day was infectious, even when heavy rain had the men huddled under a corrugated iron-roofed shelter. Most days were fine and even sunny, or maybe that is the way I remember them. There was almost continuous banter and laughter, and when the jackass developed an incredibly long appendage, the ribald witticisms were uproarious. I think that my sex education, as a thirteen-year-old, was advanced considerably during those bogland summers. I certainly received no such education from my parents.

The highlight of the day was the mid-morning 'drum up'. Boys had earlier lit little fires and now blackened billycans were stewing up the tea. The heady smell of turf smoke and strong tea has long endured in my memory of those bogland years. The midday break was longer and, perforce, more relaxed, after the invariably strong tea and crusty turnover bread with tinned salmon. I would sometimes take a break and wander up to the summit of the mountain where I could sit on a rock and stare down at the vast area of workings. The straight lines of the cuttings and parallel banks were alien intrusions on the former gentle curves and foldings of the heathery landscape, as was the hum of distant voices and the blue smoke from all the cooking fires. I don't remember, as a boy, that this invasion of a pristine place really disturbed me then. The workings were dwarfed by the rolling hills all around and the immense wilderness of the Wicklow Mountains stretched far to the south.

I went back, decades later, to revisit the site of the wartime turf workings. The access road was now nearly obscured by a dense forest of Sitka spruce, while on the open mountainside nature was softening the edges of the old bog trenches. A lush growth of heather covered the old scars in the deepest cuttings. Where the rocky sub-soil had been exposed, carpets of sphagnum moss had begun the regeneration of peat. Long grasses flourished in shallow boggy depressions where butterwort plants spread their seductive but sticky leaves to catch insects. A sea of white bog cotton spread over the wide marshy areas, fluffy stem heads waving in the wind. The only sound was from a lone skylark, spiralling high above.

At the end of the season the donkeys were brought back down to winter in Uncle Mick's field. There was one more exercise for them, however, and that was in the parish sports day. A highlight was the donkey race and the first task was to choose which animal could be the best choice for a win. I tried each one out in the field but most were hopeless: one of them insisted on going backwards. The jackass was stubborn but one of the jennies was a real prospect. She was bigger than the others and more strongly built. She seemed to enjoy the races and we often won. The densely tangled and overhanging hedge at the top of the field made a satisfactory shelter for them all through the winter months, along with a plentiful supply of hay.

I don't know whose idea it was to plant Uncle Mick's field with oats, but for one year during the war the field was ploughed, harrowed and then planted. The sprouting of young green shoots in early spring was, for me at least, the first heart-warming sign of lengthening days to come. I looked forward, even at the winter solstice, to those other 'firsts': the first swallows, the first cuckoo call, the first sticky buds on the chestnut trees, bluebells in the oak woods and, sadly now no more, the harsh *kerrx-kerrx* of the corncrake in the meadows below our house. The progress of the cornfield now became an almost daily obsession. By early summer the crop was a lushly waving sea of green, speckled with red poppies. My father then announced that the harvesting of the corn was to be my job, 'after the donkey work on the bog, of course,' he said, laughing. My initial thought was that here was another source of earnings, I could buy that weekly magazine *The War Illustrated* and satisfy the ruling passion I had in those days.

That summer's late August was especially dry and sunny, the cornfield was golden and now ripe for harvesting. It was quite a small field, so hand-cutting by scythe did not seem to be a formidable task. I was already fairly adept with the scythe to cut nettles and long grass at the sides of our vegetable plots. I could hardly wait to get started that first glorious morning but, before any work could begin, the blade had to be razor-sharp. This sharpening was essential and always a difficult task. The blade had to be honed with a whetstone and the best way to do this was to stroke the stone down each side of the cutting edge, alternating each stroke front and back. It was tiring and awkward to do this at the beginning, but I soon became more relaxed, and as the hiss of the stroking stone turned into a near singing, the cutting edge was gleaming white.

There was an almost primordial satisfaction in making the first swathe of cuts, the blade slicing through the stalks in wide sweeps. The euphoria of the early morning work, however, soon died and the labour became hard. The sun got hot, my shirt came off and sweat poured. It was a relief when my mother appeared with a bottle of cold milk and a sausage sandwich. In the afternoon a local man came in to help and by evening the cutting was done. The next stage was more backbreaking. The cut stalks had to be gathered up into sheaves that had to be tied into a neat bundle. My helper showed me how to do this with a twist of stalks he called a 'double band'. I gathered that this was a skill known only by old hands. I felt privileged and not a little smug to be given such a secret technique. The sheaves were then stacked in triangular stooks to further dry out and await carting off. It was a good day's work but I was exhausted, my back hurt and my hands were blistered. I was glad it was over.

I don't remember what happened to the oats crop. It must have been sold because we had no use for it, but we were at least partially self-sufficient during those war years. The windmill gave us electric light, although not when the wind dropped. We had a year-long stock of potatoes that were stored outdoors in a large clamp at the top of the rear garden. It was sloped to throw off rainwater and was covered with a thick blanket of straw to keep the crop fresh. Uncle Jem's vegetable plots had cabbages, carrots and onions, while fruit bushes gave us blackcurrants and redcurrants, raspberries, loganberries and gooseberries. Then there was the apple orchard. This was just one more of my mother's numerous worries. When the apples were just ripening, they were vulnerable to being raided by local boys where 'boxing the fox' was considered a traditional sport. My mother seemed to spend most of her time, before we felt it was right to pick the crop, watching out of the back windows for intruders from the mountain behind. The cows that grazed the 'long acre' were a further cross she had to bear, like the continual leaks from the flat roof over the kitchen. There was one animal, in particular, that apparently was owned by a woman who had no land of her own. She just let the cow onto the road to feed on the lush grasses along the banks. We had a wooden double gate to our driveway in those days and my mother swore that the cow could lift the gate open with one horn and then trample all over her beloved flowerbeds in the front garden. My father's comment that we could have good manure was not appreciated.

The hen house arrived one morning. This was supposed to be a surprise present from my father. My mother, however, thought otherwise. It was yet another chore for her when the hens arrived. She quickly decreed that it would have to be the responsibility of the children to look after the hens. She gave me the task of cleaning out the hen house at regular intervals. This turned out to be the most horrible job I had ever experienced. Incredible layers of hen shit coated every surface, and shovelling the place clean was a disgusting job.

'Why couldn't we just leave them in their dirt?' I complained.

'Don't be ridiculous,' I was told.

I felt like killing all the birds with my shovel.

My father's energy was restless and unbounded, particularly in the wartime years. His enterprises were so diverse that we never knew what the next venture would be. There was a morning, for instance, when one of his lorries delivered a huge collection of large wooden slatted crates, bought at some auction. These were dumped in an untidy heap at the side of our front garden and became a playground and delight for my brothers and me. One of the crates stood on the top of the pile and I decided that it would make a perfect miniature submarine. Some old wooden barrels were part of an earlier auction purchase and I took one of these and managed to cut out the bottom. This made a suitable conning tower when mounted on top of the crate. An opening was then made in the slats and we had an entry to our new adventure. The crate had a dense packing of wood shavings, which were, I supposed, used as a protective for whatever the crates originally had contained. We packed this all around the sides and made a snug hiding place for our games, as the commanders of this new vessel. After a few weeks the game was that our sub was about to be captured by the enemy and I decided to burn the secret papers. I hadn't thought about the wood shavings. We scrambled up the barrel/conning tower just before the conflagration consumed our submarine. The fire was spectacular and the entire pile of crates was reduced to ashes. My mother was more annoyed than my father, even though his supply of firewood for the winter was no more.

During one of those winters in the early years of the war there was heavy snow and freezing temperatures. I like to remember it, however, as 'The day I nearly killed de Valera'. The snow was so deep that the men of Barnacullia had to dig a narrow path all the way down from the top of the village past our house to Lamb Doyle's pub where the bread van could just reach. After a few weeks, successive melts and clearances made the road barely passable but Ryan's Hill remained an arduous barrier. It was not alone steep but a small stream overflow had created an icy surface down the centre of the slope. It was a paradise for our winter sport of sliding, or better still, for careering down the hill on a tilted-up corrugated iron make-believe toboggan. Three other local boys and I had just finished a run down from the very top of the hill when a large dark-coloured car was attempting to drive up the slope. It skidded to a stop right beside us and then slid backwards in wild swerves until the driver managed to halt the skid against a grassy bank.

Two men in dark suits got out of the car and glared at us. One of them held open the rear door and a tall, thin man, dressed in a long overcoat emerged. I recognised him at once as Eamon de Valera. He was the leader of the government, a very important man to us, as we stood there in trepidation, our mouths open, waiting for the doom that was to come. Dev looked at us and gave us a small smile. His bodyguards, as my father described them to me when I confessed our part in the near disaster, helped him to the side of the road where the snow was firm and he could continue to walk easily up to the top of the hill. My father explained that Dev often liked to walk in Barnacullia. He said that he could feel safe there, an area that was firmly Old IRA in the years of conflict.

The later years of the war were good times for my father's business. He was prospering with his turf supply project and was happy with his role in the LDF. We could now afford family holidays. The best of these was the summer month's move to the seaside resort of Skerries in north County Dublin. We rented a cottage. It was a white-painted, thatched, traditional building, as were many in that old village. There were two beaches: the north beach was cold and uninviting, while the larger south beach was, at least in my boyhood memory, always sunny. The most southerly part of the beach was largely out-of-bounds since it was reserved for the nuns from the adjacent convent. I have a memory of those Victorian bathing machines that could be wheeled down to the water's edge so that the modesty of the nuns could be preserved. We all kept well away from this section. A small peninsula poked out into the Irish Sea; it was grass-covered and fringed with rocks. At the very point, a deep pool was formed between the rocks. This was called the Captain's Pool and was reserved for men only.

It was a perfect bathing place, with rock platforms suitable for diving. As a concession, females were allowed an exclusive use of the pool for just one hour of the day. During that time, boys would gather on the rocks and make catcalls to the girls, but not if their mothers were also there. A smaller, less attractive, pool was on the southern side of the peninsula and this was designated as a females-only place.

A major attraction for the summer of 1946, my last year in school, was the start of the motorcycle race named the Skerries 100. This was a circuit of about seven miles, fourteen times, and included the main street, where the biggest crowds would gather. I had just got my own motorbike and became addicted to the race. They needed many volunteers to act as marshals in order to keep sightseers well back from potentially dangerous parts of the course. I enthusiastically volunteered with some of my friends and we were given one possibly dangerous bend to monitor. In the days that followed the race, I, along with two boys who also had bikes, secretly had our own race around the circuit. We completed just a few laps, and could only purr down Main Street at a sedate pace.

Single-sex schools were the norm in the Ireland of that time, so summer holidays in Skerries were where boys and girls could meet and young love could blossom. There was a new cinema on the seafront and a hall for all sorts of enter-tainment. On balmy summer evenings the cliff path to the south was ideal for couples to stroll down and maybe seek out a grassy hollow as dusk descended. The Church's censure of 'company keeping', however, could loom over those growing youthful desires.

I fell in love when I was seventeen, though I didn't know it at the time. It was a fairly brief relationship, desultory and ten-tative, but when it was over, I knew then what had happened.

Her name was Yvonne and she lived, for some of the year, in the old seaside village of Skerries. Her home was a small, two-storey Victorian villa perched near the beach and the start of the little peninsula. I cannot remember when we actually met and spoke to each other, but I have a clear memory of when I first saw her. It was at the Captain's bathing place during the one grudging hour granted each day to women and girls. She stood on the highest diving rock in a black bathing suit and when she took off, she entered the water like an arrow, with hardly a splash. She swam so smoothly, it was seal-like, and I was fascinated. When eventually we went together to swim, at a rocky pool away from the more popular bathing places, I was sadly aware of my own feeble efforts at diving and even of swimming. Yvonne would dive effortlessly and often swim around me like a dolphin. She would tease me about my lack of prowess, but always playfully and I never felt chastened. I just liked being with her.

I never did walk the cliff path in Skerries with Yvonne during any of those seductive July and August twilights. These evenings were not always barren, however, because after a film show I sometimes managed to persuade a girl to stroll with me along that darkening path. Eros certainly prevailed, with the coalescence of warm air, enticing summer dresses and just plain desire, over any clerical denunciations of the evils of 'company keeping'.

After the holiday's end I would visit Yvonne at her home whenever I could. It was a long journey by motor bike, right across the city, then down the main road to Belfast until the sign for Skerries appeared. A narrow, old road, past shorn cornfields, led to the seaside village settling into an early winter's calm. A pattern developed for those, albeit infrequent, visits. Yvonne would greet me warmly and we would sit down on a sofa that faced a window to the north beach. Invariably, she would curl up at one end of the sofa while I, at the other end, would turn to face her. It was always the same: I remember how she would fix me with her gaze, from that round and laughing face. Our talk was always about trivialities, never anything remotely serious. I don't recall a single thought we shared but remember well how I loved our times together.

We did meet once in the city. Yvonne was still a schoolgirl, while I had just started college. She was in her final year at Alexandra, an all-girls' school that happened to be located directly opposite the main building of University College Dublin. She sent me a note stating that one of the projects she had to complete for her final examination was to host a formal dinner party, along with a small team of fellow students. The project consisted of everything from the menu choice to the preparation, the presentation and then to the conduct of the feast. Each student would be required to have a male partner for the dinner party and Yvonne asked me if I would be hers for the evening.

I accepted the invitation at once, although the prospect was daunting. I was eighteen and, even though Yvonne was nearly two years younger, I always felt she was ahead of me in many ways. She was sharp and witty and could tease me unmercifully in conversation. I could be sometimes awkward and clumsy when with her but inevitably she made me feel completely at ease. The invitation to a special dinner party was exciting at one level, although I dreaded doing the wrong thing. I had never been to a dinner party. My mother never rose to such an event; she was not a great cook in any case. I had never been to a fancy restaurant. Would I know which piece of cutlery I should pick up first, for instance? Was there a possibility that my graceless or potential clumsiness could spoil my dinner partner's score in the exam? Or what if I did not even know when to sit down or to stand up, for heaven's sake. I was becoming more and more apprehensive about the whole looming affair.

Yvonne met me on the evening before the event and assured me that she and her team of fellow students were the ones whose performance was to be judged. The dinner partners were irrelevant she said, in her habitual caustic dismissal of my fears. 'You're just there for decoration' was her departing quip. I quite liked the idea of being just a decoration.

The dining table at the school was a splendid sight. The linen tablecloth was dazzlingly white with two silver branched candlesticks in the centre. Wine glasses were sparkling but the dreaded cutlery was in abundance at each place. The diners were introduced to one another and, more formally, to the teacher, who took her seat at the head of the table. She was the one who would judge the event and award marks. I was in awe at first but quickly realised that the other male partners were just as uncomfortable as I was. The whole company soon relaxed and a little banter, mainly started by Yvonne, eased the formality. The cutlery was not a problem. Yvonne kicked me on the shin if my hand hovered over the wrong implement. I have no memory whatsoever of the food. I was no epicure anyway; my mother used a lot of tinned peas. The glittering wine glasses were for show only, because lemonade was the main potion. The female diners were still schoolgirls, while the males, all students, were far too unrefined and impecunious to take to serious wine drinking. Yvonne told me afterwards that the dinner party was a huge success and that she and her team had got a first-rate pass.

Our last time together was on an afternoon in winter, some two years from that summer's day when we first met.

Skerries was like a ghost town when I arrived. Holiday homes were empty and shuttered while the sea off the north beach was lustreless, sullen even, with a slow, oily swell. We sat on the couch with the window framing cold white waves. This time Yvonne did not sit in her usual curled up fashion at one end but now sat close to me. The conversation was the same, however: inconsequential chit-chat. There was a moment of silence, which after the chatter seemed interminable but was probably only a few seconds. Suddenly she turned to me and said, 'Sean, I'm going to marry Robert.'

I didn't feel it as a bombshell, because she had often talked about Robert and I knew they were close, but that stark and simple statement left me without words. Although the conversation continued for a while, we both knew that everything had changed. On the ride back home in drizzly rain and early darkness, I realised that not only was it all over for Yvonne and me, but that she *was* my first love after all.

Years passed and I had largely forgotten those seaside days when I was young. A couple of short and largely frustrating liaisons filled the following student months and then I met Nuala. All changed. I was smitten by this lissome nineteen-year-old, who soon became my life partner. The following decade was a whirl of activity: the hectic creative work of a young architect; three years of exciting times of work and exploration for both of us in East Africa; then dark days, the trauma of the death of our second baby, soon followed by the shock of the murder of our closest friend.

Back in Ireland, life settled into a time of comparative calm. I was returning one day from a visit to a new building project in County Cavan when I saw a group of large shiny trailers parked on the edge of a fairgreen. On an impulse, I stopped and suddenly thought of Yvonne. I vaguely recalled that she was marrying into a theatrical family. I wondered if this was a travelling theatre, one of the last of the so-called 'fit-ups'? I enquired at one of the units, using her married name, and was told that yes, she was in the trailer at the end. She was the same, a little older, as was I, but the same bubbly person with that well-remembered laughing face. She told me that she took small parts in the plays they performed throughout the summer season and I shared a little of my life since we had last met. Our meeting was brief but warm: it rekindled memories of both the joys and woes of those far-off summer days, but I knew they were only memories, soon to fade away.

One afternoon Nuala told me that a colleague from the clinic where they both worked, who was a friend of Yvonne's family, had told her that Yvonne was ill and in hospital. The friend had been to see her several times and in the course of one conversation Yvonne talked nostalgically about her young days in Skerries. She mentioned my name and that she would like to see me again. 'Why not go and visit her?' Nuala said.

It was a sudden surprise and my emotions were mixed. At one level I disliked intensely the idea of hospital visits and always avoided any discussion about illnesses. At a deeper level, however, I knew that Yvonne was still in my memory. My thought was that 'old love never dies', a cliché perhaps, but there it was, after all those years. I just said, 'Maybe. I'll think about it.'

I was shocked when I saw her. Her face was blotched and puffed and when I bent down to kiss her, trying to avoid the blotches, I felt as clumsy as I did in those early years. The laughing face may have gone but there was the old sparkle in her eyes and she had the same vivacious voice. She did not speak about her illness and I did not enquire. It seemed more comfortable that way. It was easy to slip back into the old pattern of idle chat. That way I did not have to face the obvious truth that she was seriously ill. Her room had a window opening out to the west, with a view of the hills and a golf course in the foreground. I found my gaze increasingly straying to the view: lines of soldiery poplars, the manicured green fairways and my own beloved, distant Three Rock Mountain. I found it hard to focus on Yvonne's ravaged face. When it was time to leave, she told me that she was being discharged in a week and would return home to convalesce. 'Will you come to visit?' she said.

'Of course' was my reply, but deep down I dreaded facing the fact of her condition. There was such deterioration from that lively and vivacious figure I remembered so well, standing on a rock and about to dive into the pool. Our good-byes were warm but I could feel nothing but a deep sadness as I left her.

My office was quite near where Yvonne lived: a quiet inner suburban road, tree-lined and close to a small park. Her home was one of a little terrace of Victorian two-storey houses set well back from the roadway. After a quick lunch at the office, the short walk through the park was a pleasure. It was early spring and I always remember the large chestnut tree at the park entrance where I watched for that first real sign of a season's change, the sticky buds all ready to open. When I lifted the latch on the little iron gate, I could see Yvonne at one of the upper windows: she would wave to me and the buzzer on the door allowed me enter. Our greeting, for me at least, was somewhat perfunctory. I had not yet adapted to that physical change in her. It never took long, however, for me to slip back into that old warm and agreeable mood whenever I was with her. She often produced photograph albums; we would look through them together and reminisce about those early days in Skerries. The visits were brief, never more than an hour, and the good-byes were always the same: a peck on the cheek and a short embrace.

The weeks went by and my visits became routine and each time more congenial. Her illness was never mentioned. She did not speak about it and I never asked. At one level I was afraid to ask. In truth, I found it easier to avoid bad news, in any situation. She rarely mentioned Robert and I had the feeling that they were separated, perhaps amicably. Spring was well advanced, the chestnut tree was flaunting its white candles and I was now looking forward to our weekly meetings. It was a sunny day when I opened the garden gate and saw her waving at the upper window. She had habitually worn a quite ordinary but comfortable dressing gown because she was still supposed to have lots of bed rest. She was in a particularly radiant mood and had changed into a white, lacy peignoir. Just before I left, she turned to me and said, 'You know, Sean, you and I should have married.'

I had no words to reply. Our farewell embrace was not the usual perfunctory one but now was warm and close. I saw her wave to me again as I closed the garden gate and walked back through the park. I thought of what she had just said and of the wistful tone of those few words. I could only feel touched: my life, after all, with Nuala and our young family was happy and settled and I felt no regrets.

It was only a few days later that Robert phoned me and told me that Yvonne had died. I had expected this all along but preferred not to think about the possibility. I realised that her bright and breezy optimism when we were together was her way of easing her last few months of life. I, on the other hand, could not face the fact that she was dying. Robert told me about the funeral arrangements and I thanked him and said that I would be there.

I took my seat near the rear of the church. I felt like an outsider. Except for Robert, I had never met other members of Yvonne's family or any of her other friends. I found it hard to look at the coffin, staring instead at the stained-glass windows, and I hardly heard a word of the service. It was less than ten years since those two visits to the cemetery off the Jinja Road in Kampala – a story I would write about later. We had then been living in East Africa, and having just lost a baby son, followed shortly by the killing of one of our closest friends, the feelings of loss were overwhelming.

It was the same at the burial. I could only stand apart from the main body of mourners gathered at the graveside. I walked away quickly at the end, avoiding the inevitable polite sharing, but in the main to hide my sadness. I did resolve, however, to return and visit Yvonne's grave some day when I could be alone.

I did not go back for many years. It was only by accident I found myself driving past the cemetery, a route I had not used since that day. On impulse, I turned and found a place to park and walked up the avenue of yew trees to find her grave. I was glad that it was in the older section with few of those ugly, shiny black monuments. It was a simple gravestone, a slab of granite, her name at the top and the dates: 1930–1966. She was too young to die.

My father bought a hut in Shankill in the late 1940s. It was near the beach and, ostensibly, was to be another place for the family to have summer holidays when the Skerries month was over. The hut was wooden and painted green. The more grandiose title of chalet was applied to these seaside dwellings in much later and more prosperous times. I have only two memories of the hut, both incidents that must have happened while I was still at school. I remember finding a packet of cigarettes there, partly hidden behind a drawer. I had never smoked and here was a temptation. Outside the door I smoked two cigarettes and promptly turned a shade of green to match the hut. For most of the rest of the day I was so sick that I wanted to die.

The second incident was to remain in my memory for a lifetime. I was with my brothers Eamon and Brian on the beach, and the three of us were deeply engaged in a construction project of sorts, a dam of sand and stones against the slowly incoming tide perhaps. In any case we were free, out in the wide open, a blue, blue sky and an endless horizon. There was a distant shout and we turned to see a figure standing on top of the steps leading down to the beach. It was our father and when we drew nearer we heard him say, 'School starts tomorrow.' It was like a sentence of death. Our time of freedom was over and the concrete schoolyard of Synge Street would now draw us in again. I think that vision of my father calling out those three words became fixed in my memory. Was it a metaphor for all those future unpleasant deadlines, which soon must be faced?

I left school in 1946. My last terms in Synge Street Secondary were so different from those early years, when entry to that schoolyard could fill me with trepidation or even dread. That fearful and lonely eleven-year-old, fresh from the mountain, was only a memory. I was now confident and had a lust for life. I had close friends, Brother Arnold's art classes were a joy each Wednesday and those wonderful English classes were always a pleasure. As seniors, we had the measure of the oppressors, who could no longer intimidate us. But most of all I had conquered that yard. Roaring through the gate each morning on my BSA 500 puffed me up for the day. Leaving each afternoon was even better, when I triumphantly rode off home.

The last paper of my final exam was calculus, a subject I hated like poison, and I knew that I would fail it miserably. I was confident that I had done well in all the other papers, so I did something I had never done before. I skipped the day of the exam. There would be no sanction from the school: those schooldays were over for good. I was a free spirit at last. My father decided to celebrate my freedom with a cycling expedition to Courtown Harbour in County Wexford. With my two brothers and my father, we set off happily on a glorious summer's day for the long ride to a seaside hotel where we were to spend a few nights. We had never stayed in a hotel, so this was to be a first and worth every mile of that journey.

When we arrived at last, surprise, surprise, whom did we see? It was Miss Grace. What a coincidence was my thought. It never occurred to me then to think about the allocation of rooms for us in that hotel. I did however wonder about it later. Many years after that trip Brian said to me, 'Did you not know that the hut in Shankill was father's love nest for him and Gracie?' I was a lot more naïve than my younger brother. I suppose that deep down my wariness with Miss Grace (Gracie was my father's name for her) was a sign of my unease; that, perhaps, she was more than his secretary. She rarely spoke to me or I to her, and the distance between us certainly widened after that trip to Courtown Harbour.

I won a scholarship to university from my final exam. It was to University College Dublin, and I opted to study architecture. Before I left Synge Street, my father had a plan, or maybe just an idea, that I should go into the business of providing sound and recording equipment for musical performances. This was already one of his many enterprises. When I told him that I wanted to go to university, he did not express any disappointment; instead, he was fully supportive. I think that my parents, neither of whom had had the privilege of second-level schooling, were secretly proud to have me go to university.

On the appointed day I arrived at Earlsfort Terrace to register for my chosen course. I was too early and, while waiting around outside the main building, I met another putative architecture student. We chatted for a while and decided to walk in St Stephen's Green to kill time. We met another would-be student walking towards the college and he happened to be an acquaintance of my new-found friend. He asked what course we favoured and when we both said Architecture, he said, 'I'll go for that so.' That's the way it was in those far-off days. My scholarship was £80 a year, subject to passing each year's exam. The university fee was £17 and my mother kept the rest.

I have no idea how the profession of architecture came so easily to my mind. I was well into my second year's exams in the School of Architecture when I became friends with Uinsean McEoin. He was much older and had already qualified as an architect. I think I got to know him through the newly formed Irish Mountaineering Club. Uinsean was already a formidable mountain walker, in addition to becoming one of the first Irish architectural conservationists. He told me that the early eighteenth-century Rothery family of architects, John Rothery and his son Isaac, had designed the austerely beautiful Mount Ievers at Sixmilebridge, County Clare. Years later I asked Edward MacLysaght, the famous genealogist, about my name and asked if these Rotherys might have been distant relatives. He said yes, of course, and that there were numerous examples of occupations reappearing in later generations. My paternal grandfather was John and I had a grand-uncle Isaac. There was a tradition of stone-carving in my family and the eighteenth-century Bury Monument, a stone sculpture in the Church of Ireland in Adare, County Limerick is signed Rothery.

The School of Architecture in UCD was, for me, another world, in comparison to the disciplined, almost custodial, regime at Synge Street. The studio for the junior students was a vast, high and top-lit space filled with lines of plain wooden benches. This was to be our home base for the next two years. The school occupied the upper floor of the remaining parts of the old University and Exhibition Building, now hidden behind the new, early twentieth-century limestone block on Earlsfort Terrace. The greatest change, for that fresh intake in October 1946, was a new freedom after the repressive authority of schooldays. We could come and go as we pleased, although, as some were to discover, authority could rule in more subtle ways in the university world. Those early days, however, were, for me at least, hugely enjoyable in that crowded and somewhat ramshackle studio. We were, perhaps, a little subdued, even slightly overawed, by the new surroundings, but the atmosphere soon changed. We could wander around to the benches of others, exchange opinions, and the whole room sometimes would explode in laughter or banter, particularly if no teacher was present. The other big change was the new reality of a male and female body of students, a real novelty after years of single-sex schooling.

Venus de Milo stood at the top of the staircase, welcoming us each morning into the school. She must have been there for quite a long time, probably since the foundation of the school, because she was covered in rubber stampings. These were usually the official stamps of the school, necessary for the submission of completed drawings. She was a plaster cast, one of many other, largely decrepit, casts scattered around the school: cast-offs, senior students told us scornfully, from the National College of Art. These seniors, third years and fourth years, were housed in smaller studios; cheap wooden partitions gave privacy to these superior beings. A smaller room at the top of the stairs was furnished with large ceramic sinks; this was also the domain of Arthur. He was a diminutive figure but an imposing presence, despite his size and habitual brown work coat. He was a slightly intimidating presence to the fresh intake, at least for the first few weeks. Some of the more timid newcomers even thought he was the professor, because he seemed to know everything. Arthur was actually just the attendant; his main responsibility was to collect the finished drawing projects, storing them for the teachers to mark. We were soon made aware, by the seniors naturally, that it was important to keep on his good side. We had not met the real professor yet.

Each new student was allocated a bench space and a couple of bricks. The function of these was soon obvious. It involved our spanking new double elephant drawing board, T square and set square, which were the tools of our future trade. I remember our first lesson: how to prop up the drawing board with the two bricks and how to use the T square and set square. That lesson seemed absurdly obvious, but the set projects would challenge us in the days to come.

The studio was our home, our base. Unlike many other courses in university at that time, where students would move between lectures sometimes aimlessly, and where the library was the usual option. We, on the other hand, were bound to the studio and the core work and continuous assessments of the projects that were crucial to our passing through each year. I was in my element, however. I loved drawing and here was an opportunity to indulge all day in my favourite activity. Our first assignment was to draw each letter of the Roman alphabet, an exercise that seemed to make no sense at first, but soon the beauty and perfection of these ancient letters were plain to see.

I think that we all learned more from each other than we did from any teaching at the time. This was minimal and sporadic. Our teacher was only part-time and he was given the somewhat less than impressive title of Demonstrator. Co-operation soon became an essential part of studio life. After the intense and concentrated effort of completing the line drawing, a carnival atmosphere would erupt. This was the time of 'Application of the Wash'. Our drawing would not be totally finished until it was rendered. This could be applied in Chinese ink or more commonly in watercolour. A well-loaded fat watercolour brush was then used to start the wash, from the top and evenly spread across the sheet. This was a time of extreme tension and could be followed by cries of ecstasy or wails of disaster. A daring element grew as some of us became more expert at the wash application and this was by the addition of lots of sediment into the mix. This produced a mottled texture to the grading but it could be a dangerous sortie to attempt. A fail in the project was the price of a rendering disaster.

When the finished sheet was handed up and stamped, there was a short time to relax. On one of these days my beloved new double elephant board vanished from the studio, probably when the class was out attending a lecture. I was shocked but soon found that other raw first years had the same problem. The more senior students usually had several drawing boards in action at the same time; the senior projects normally had numerous sheets of drawings to complete a single project. The innocent first year was seen as a rich source for extra boards. What was I to do? A drawing board was indispensable for an architectural student and I just couldn't afford to buy a new one.

I had not dared, nor indeed had any of us in those first months of the course, to enter any of the three senior year studios. I was desperate, however, and decided to go in search of my property, but I waited until I thought the older students might have left their places, at lunchtime or morning breaks, for instance. The third-year studio was just outside our own big space and since it was open to the gallery, I could see that it was deserted. A quick look of the boards, some on the benches and more stacked against the walls, did not yield mine. The fourth year was a forbidden place, partitioned and with a con-stantly closed door. I took a chance and quietly entered. It was not empty: three people were sitting at their drawings and each stared silently at this intruder. There were a number of spare boards stacked against the partitions and I steeled myself, I hoped casually, to see if one of them had my name carved on the back. The three seniors watched me for a few minutes, then one of them, a tall, mature-looking individual who, to my eyes, was extremely well dressed, stood and strolled over to me.

'What are you looking for, young man?' he said.

'I am trying to find my drawing board' was my reply.

He took me by the elbow and gently if firmly steered me towards the door, saying in an amused tone, 'Fourth years do not steal drawing boards.' The door was closed behind me and I was ignominiously banished.

I told my story to the others in our studio and there was indignant talk of a raid on the senior studios to recover our property, but caution prevailed. We were learning a little more each day of the absolute power the college authorities had for discipline.

I bided my time, however, and was not going to give up on my search. I checked the fourth-year studio one day at lunch-time and, finding it empty, swiftly scanned the stacked boards. No sign of mine but another caught my eye. It had a name carved on the back in huge letters painted black. The name was Dan O'Herlihy. I grabbed it and tore back to my bench.

It was already a famous name in the School of Architecture. Dan O'Herlihy graduated in 1944 with a B.Arch but almost straightaway left the profession and went into acting. He was impressive in theatre in Dublin and, as a result, was spotted for what became a long and successful career in film and later television roles. One of his first films was *Odd Man Out*, which was screened in 1947, the year after I entered the school. He played the lead in Luis Buñuel's *The Adventures of Robinson Crusoe* in 1954 and eventually starred in nearly forty films. I jealously guarded his drawing board throughout my five years in the School of Architecture, leaving it behind for some new student to use, just as he did – a windfall and a lifesaver for me.

The drawing projects for those early weeks in first year necessitated rigorous and exacting draughtsmanship and little opportunity for individual creativity. For relief from this arduous task, however, every now and then a one-day project was introduced. It was called a Sketch Design, and a free style drawing or painting was acceptable. I think that the title of the first of these one-day sketch projects was 'Design for a Monument to a Fallen Soldier'.

We had hardly begun to get to know all our fellow students by this time. There were up to forty of us in the year, and so far no one individual stood out as an exceptional talent. The studio was a buzz of activity and most of us, but not all, were excited at the prospect of letting our hair down, so to speak, in some carefree expression. Some, however, found the task to be daunting. We had barely begun to work when we noticed that one student, who up to now had just shown solid conformity in his work, was donning an artist's smock. He then produced an impressive wooden box filled with tubes of oil paints, several brushes and, most extraordinary of all, a painter's palette. To crown the spectacle, he took out a curly pipe, filled it with tobacco, which he lit and then began to paint, through clouds of blue fragrant smoke. We were transfixed. For some of us the question was: is this the ideal to which we must strive to reach but which will lead to hopeless despair for others? He would go on to be far and away the leading exponent of beautiful drawing and all other design works in the five years in the school.

The professor came into our studio some weeks after our first day. When I say 'came' it was more like a sudden appearance or even an apparition. One moment the studio was buzzing with chatter and song, then a sudden silence. 'It's the prof,' somebody whispered, and there he was. He was a small, dapper figure, dressed in an impeccable suit and tie: a stark contrast to the scruffiness of us students. He moved silently around the benches, some slight glances at drawings in progress and, except for a smile or two, uttered no verbal exchange. And then he was gone.

Professor Joseph Vincent Downes was a fairly recent appointment to the post and a personality far removed from his predecessor, the grandiloquently named Rudolf Maximilian Butler. We knew little of this, however, but we did know all about his car. It was an Armstrong Siddeley, a lime green colour, and it was always spotlessly clean. On sunny days Downes would invariably move it from the rear to the front of the college or from wherever the sunshine could cloud the paintwork. It was a luxurious car. We had never seen anything like it. Dublin in the late 1940s was a sea of old Fords and bicycles.

In my five years in the UCD School of Architecture I cannot remember ever speaking to Downes or he to me, except for one word that I recall with gratitude. It was an oral examination at the end of one year where an external examiner was an important part of the inquisition, as we called it. My extern that year was the Professor of Architecture from the Liverpool School, a dour pedant. He barked a question at me that sounded like, 'What is a wailey?' I was open-mouthed, dumbstruck. What is he talking about? Then my professor, in his gentle voice, said 'wayleave', and I was off the scaffold. I have never forgotten his kindness.

The professor's one class with us in that first year was called the Colour Circle. This was an undemanding drawing exercise, using poster paint to create a circle of related colours. I doubt if any of us, at that time at least, saw the point of the exercise. His near ghostly appearance in our first-year studio that morning would typify the extent of his presence in the school. It was un-remarkable and it would be hard to say that he had any special influence on the work of the students.

It was all the more astonishing, for me particularly, to discover decades later that J.V. Downes was indeed a remark-able man. He travelled widely in the 1920s and 1930s; he was a superb photographer and one of the earliest, if not the earliest, maker of films on architecture; and he lectured regularly about contemporary architecture to his peers in the Royal Institute of Architects of Ireland and to the Architectural Association. Downes left behind an impressive archive of black and white glass slides of buildings, which comprised images of great European monuments and also impressive international ex-amples of pioneering modern architecture. He subscribed to most of the influential British and foreign language architec-tural journals, and volumes of these were professionally bound yearly and kept in the library of his practice, Downes and Mee-han, at 53 Fitzwilliam Square, Dublin. I cannot recall that any of his undoubted erudition was passed on to my generation of architecture students.

The Emergency ended in 1945 and the universities began to receive a steady stream of demobbed young men from the forces. These ex-servicemen were awarded grants from the British government to attend university, and Irish institutions were also included in the places eligible. Our first year of architecture in UCD had one notable entrant from that coterie of war veterans. His name was W.B. Kirkwood-Hackett. I never remember ever hearing his forename; we always knew him by his initials. He had been a member of the Royal Air Force, where he was a rear gunner in Bomber Command. He was awarded the distinction of the Distinguished Flying Cross, one of the highest medals for bravery in the British military.

W.B. always seemed to wear his blue RAF greatcoat, even in the studio, but this could have been to keep him warm. The big room, with its glazed roof, could be cold and draughty, but I rather think that he found it hard to part from his uniformed past. Most of us were more than a little in awe of him and his history, and that left something of a barrier between him and the main body of fellow students. W.B. may have been only a couple of years older than the rest of us, but in regard to his experiences there was an immense gulf between him and those of us just out of secondary school.

There was an early incident that caused a serious rift in any growing friendships between W.B. and the rest of us. We would each need to print our name on completed drawings that were to be handed up for marking. Kirkwood-Hackett always added DFC to his own name on his submissions, but one day, an individual, thinking it was funny, changed the F into a P, making it read as DPC. This was the short for Damp Proof Course, learned from our early lectures on Building Construction. The veteran airman reacted with incandescent rage and said what he thought of the anonymous perpetrator. Many of us might have thought of it as funny, but with more than a little guilt. His reaction compounded this greatly and I think that all of us were ashamed. We were, after all, a bunch of schoolboys and schoolgirls, while he was a war hero.

I remember speaking to W.B. some time later when he opened up to talk of his wartime exploits. He had won the DFC for a pioneering bomber night raid far into Nazi Germany, an operation where many of his friends and fellow airmen died. He was a rear gunner and he told me that the rear gunner was called Arse Hole Charlie by the rest of the crew because it was considered the most dangerous place to be in any aircraft. I thought of this afterwards. He would be sitting crouched in a tiny Perspex bubble that must have felt like being out in dark space. When crossing the continental coast, the searchlights would stab the sky and soon the anti-aircraft guns would send blossoming explosions all around the formations. The rear gunner would have the added fear of watching for the night fighters and the inevitable lethal stream of fiery tracer. No wonder he hated us for that idiotic prank. As a former fellow student, John O'Reilly, said to me in later years, 'Many of us were in short trousers when he was up there near death.'

Kirkwood-Hackett had a difficult few years, however, more from authority than from student juvenile japes. His grant from the British government was dependent on his passing all subjects each year, as was mine from my County Council scholarship. He failed in just one subject, a minor one in the first year of the course. His grant was refused and he appealed on the grounds that the subject was a very small part of the whole body of work that had to be approved. His appeal appeared to succeed and he continued into the second year of the course. He again failed just one other subject, also a minor one, but this time he did not manage to have his grant restored. The college authorities refused to allow him to continue his studies and so he left the course. Most of us thought he had been shabbily treated, both by the bureaucratic and despotic university bosses but even more so by the British administrators of the grant system. They had little sympathy for the young men, many heroes, whose lives had been changed utterly by that war. As for the rest of us students, it was plain that we also had few rights in those days, so keeping your head down was the way to survive.

Before W.B. departed, however, he did have one final triumph. One morning in the Physics Theatre, Professor John Nolan was just leaving after his usual lecture when the College Chaplain, Father McKernan, barged in for his occasional short homily. He was always sure of a captive audience because we were all too docile in those days to dare to leave and thus challenge his clerical authority. This time his talk was more of a harangue than a religious discourse. He was angry and we students were all to blame.

'If you don't come to my sodality,' he thundered, 'don't come to me expecting a reference.'

We listened in silence, but then W.B., who was sitting in his usual seat at the end of the top row, stood up and slowly walked down the steps. He was wearing his habitual RAF blue greatcoat and as he began to walk slowly towards the door to the right of the rostrum, McKernan, who had fallen silent as W.B. rose from his seat, spoke out in a loud and hectoring tone, 'Where do you think you are going?'

Kirkwood-Hackett turned to face the prelate and in a calm and measured voice said, 'I am not of your persuasion.'

McKernan, momentarily stunned, quickly recovered and as W.B. turned his back and continued towards the door he hastily said, 'That is all right then. You may leave.'

We were all mute during this exchange and listened with bated breath to the confrontation. It was one that I doubt any of the rest of us would have dared to provoke in those days of clerical absolutism. Much later, a few of us discussed this 'Battle of the Physics Theatre' and how it was a decisive victory for our fellow student, the decorated war hero. My own thought was that this man had stared at death many times in dark skies over Germany and could have had only contempt for petty authoritarians.

After W.B. Kirkwood-Hackett left the school, he was hired by a specialised metalwork operation in Dublin. I encountered him several times after I graduated, when I was a young architect in the famous firm of Michael Scott. I thought that he was quite happy in his job but often wondered if he felt that his School of Architecture time had been cruelly cut short.

Once a week we had a session in the Physics Theatre and I doubt that any of us actually enjoyed the experience. The lecturer was Johnny Nolan, as we called the professor. The protocol seemed to be fixed as regards where the students sat. The subject of physics, for first years at least, was essential for many of the different courses. The lecture theatre, therefore, had to accommodate a wide diversity of students. This was done by grading the tiered seating in order of the perceived importance of the subject in the particular course. The exception to this, however, appeared to be that the first two rows were reserved for student priests and nuns. The architecture students were banished to the last row as the least important, we assumed. I doubt if any of us were concerned. Most of us found the lectures tedious in the extreme, reminding us too often of those school days, now far behind. We spent the time sketching and fretting over our current design project.

The National College of Art was a huge disappointment to me. We trooped down to the college once a week, a building sandwiched uncomfortably between the National Library and the grandiose Leinster House. It looked as if it was just housed in a leftover space. As we entered, we were confronted with a large plaster cast of a naked man and two naked boys wrestling with huge snakes. It was explained to us later that this was a replica of the famous ancient Greek sculpture Laocoön and his Sons, and that it was an allegory for suffering. How apt for us green architecture students, entering those doors for the first time.

The initial task handed down to us was to draw from a cast of a lion's head. It was the most uninspiring object one could imagine. It brought me right back to the 'cursèd teapot' of Miss O'Neill's class in St Mary's National School. The lion seemed to be leering at us, its face surrounded by a dusty tangle of plaster hairy mane, a torture to draw. There often seemed to be a feeling with us that architecture students were not very welcome in the domain of genuine artists. I have no memory of any other projects in the College of Art; there were equally boring plaster casts I am sure, but later in the year we were at last allowed a live model to draw.

For some inexplicable reason, however, we were only allowed a male model. This, of course, was a rumour; there was no official announcement of a restriction. We were, after all, a class of both male and female students. When the male model took off his robe and settled into his pose, he was revealed not to be completely naked but to have a tiny pouch covering his genitals. We heard afterwards that this was called a posing pouch. When I considered that Laocoön and his Sons were each flagrantly displaying their total nudity, I wondered about this need for modesty. The life drawing class was, however, a real opportunity to learn new drawing techniques and at last to feel stretched in rendering the subtle gradations of light and shade.

My appetite for more free drawing time could be satisfied only by personally enrolling for night classes in life drawing at the National College of Art. For one night a week I felt that I could advance my techniques far more than in the quite boring School of Architecture sessions.

My teachers were Maurice MacGonigal and Seán Keating. At this time, in the late 1940s, these were two of the most important artists in the Royal Hibernian Academy, albeit firm denunciators of Modernism in art. This didn't matter at all in the life drawing classes. The night students were a cheery and enthusiastic band and I mostly enjoyed my time there. After the models settled into their poses, we were often left alone to work. Our models were both male and female with not a pouch or fig leaf in sight. When MacGonigal did his rounds of the drawing pads, he was usually calm and only mildly critical of individual efforts, but Keating was a different proposition. He was often overbearing and loud in belittling any effort, line or shading that was not up to his exacting standard. He would push me aside, grab my pencil and start to draw all over my work. This annoyed me intensely and I failed to appreciate that here was a master draughtsman at work. I should have kept his drawings and long after regretted that, in my annoyance, I must have destroyed them.

The first-year studio was our home base and we spent most of our time there, but each week this essential design and drawing time was continually interrupted by quick trips to and from various lectures in the college. On top of these almost daily disconnections, in the first two years at least, there were weekly visits, not just to the College of Art in Kildare Street but also to the College of Science in Upper Merrion Street – now Government Buildings – where we had lectures in Chemistry and Engineering.

Our lecturer in Engineering was the redoubtable Thomas Garland, principal of one of the top engineering firms in Ireland. It was barely four years since the D-Day invasion of France in the closing stages of World War II. Engineering played a major part in the success of that great adventure. We learned later that the inventive ingenuity of Tommy, as we affectionally called him, played a large part in the production of the Mulberry Harbour. These were huge, reinforced concrete caissons which were towed across the English Channel and then, rising and falling with the tide, were anchored to create a temporary harbour and breakwater on the French coast.

Tommy was famous for delivering his lectures at breakneck speed and these, for me at least, were often incomprehensible. He would ignore his student class, to the extent that we could go to sleep and he would either not notice or not care. His outdoor demonstrations in surveying in Merrion Square were, however, highly enjoyable and excellent learning experiences, especially for me in my forays to archaeological digs.

The one subject I really enjoyed and later embraced was Archaeology. The professor was Seán P. O'Riordan, a warm and genial man who had a huge and abiding enthusiasm for his discipline. When I heard about the Archaeological Society, I promptly joined. Its principal activity was the field trip. Professor O'Riordan always led these outings and his project was to explore parts of the counties surrounding Dublin and to find traces of archaeological interest as yet unrecorded. The way he proposed to do this was to look at the old six-inch black and white maps that covered most of the country. These were highly detailed: individual field boundaries made it easy to locate any feature that could invite inspection. The old maps were an explorer's dream, depicting old footpaths, quarry holes and, best of all, the myriad of already recorded archaeological monuments. Each individual sheet would show the location of a dolmen, a ruined castle or its possible site, an ancient cross, a cist – a box-shaped burial chamber – along with the date of a find, a Giant's Grave, usually a Neolithic stone burial site. We would visit each of these known monuments but the mysterious earthworks, marked with tiny hachuring – shadings to show gradients – were of most interest to the scholars in the society.

The members of the UCD Archaeological Society were a motley crew – with a handful of architecture students like myself and a sprinkling of students from other disciplines – but the main body consisted of professional archaeologists, some from the National Museum and others involved in the activity of surveys and real digs. The first and obvious attraction of these outings for me was the sheer pleasure of the outdoors; climbing a grassy hill to poke around a tree-covered earthwork and hear the experts arguing about its possible date or original function. Sometimes these debates would get quite heated, but because we were all in the one club, a grudging consensus would emerge.

Seán P. was always good-humoured and he told me once about a dispute over a visiting German professor's theory on the origin of headland forts, or maybe it was the possible landing of Romans on the east coast of Ireland. He said, 'Sean, archaeology often isn't about the science. It's more a continual vendetta.'

We would usually try to find a sheltered spot for our tea break after a vigorous morning's expedition. The Volcano Kettle was then produced. This old and ingenious affair consisted of a pyramidal tin with a double skin forming a narrow cavity all around. The centre was a hollow space, which was then filled with twigs, leaves, paper or any dried combustible material. Water was then poured into the cavity and the fire was lit. In what seemed like minutes, the volcano lived up to its name and the water boiled. Tea in a billycan tasted much like my early drum up on the mountain bog. The talk was good, jokes were shared, and college gossip was aired as we stretched out on a grassy bank in early spring sunshine or huddled under the shelter of a stone wall from a bitter wind.

We once used a map that covered most of my own neighbourhood. My grandmother's field was marked, as I expected, but, to my surprise, our house was also delineated, tucked close to the field's northern boundary. This meant that this particular map had been surveyed and printed after 1930 when our house was built. There was only one other house marked in the fields as far as Lamb Doyle's pub.

On the slope of Two Rock mountain above Glencullen there was a Giant's Grave, as it was named in antique lettering. This antiquity was of particular interest to the Archaeological Society because one of our prominent members was Ruairi de Valera, son of Eamon de Valera. His major project at the time was the excavation of this site and its listing as a megalithic tomb. This relatively small area was rich in antiquities, with at least three dolmens, a hilltop cairn/tumulus, several castles, ruined churches and a cross. We visited all these and discovered several more antiquities that were not mapped.

The highlight of my time in the Archaeological Society was taking part in one of the earliest excavations in Lough Gur, County Limerick. I was pleased to be picked for the team and happily looked forward to the prospect of carefully scraping through layers of antiquity and unearthing some new and exciting evidence of ancient history. This was not to be, however, and the real reason for me being chosen was my assumed expertise in the use of the surveying level. An additional reason, I should have guessed, was my ability to make ink drawings of found objects, house sites and contoured earthworks. Not being allowed to be part of the digging team was a bitter disappointment to me, but the professor assured me that my particular skills were valuable. I grudgingly accepted my lot but felt that squinting through a surveying level and having to sit in a tent to complete a drawing was a lot more boring than the satisfying and creative work in the architectural studio.

Lough Gur, however, had a particular and haunting beauty. The surface of the lake always seemed to have a stillness, one that perhaps spoke of that Neolithic past when an ancient people lived out their lives on the slopes above the water.

The mid-morning break was a time to relax and, if we could afford it, go for coffee or tea at 86 St Stephen's Green. We could walk to this UCD house from the Earlsfort Terrace building through the beautiful, if somewhat neglected, Iveagh Gardens. The cost of a coffee and bun every day was well beyond my budget so, in good weather, a sprawl on a grassy bank in the sunshine was a pleasure I always relished.

When we left the studio for a break, we would often pass one of the large rooms on the ground floor. At break time, this room was reserved for the student priests and the door was always open, before the large body of uniformly black-clad youths appeared. However, it was the long table laid out in the centre of the room that provoked extreme envy. It was a cornucopia. We could only lust after the pile of cream buns – the luscious ones from the Monument Creamery – and dream of biting into one and licking the squashed cream from our lips. It was a morning torture. The habitual joker from our year suggested that a few of us should borrow black outfits and casually saunter in with the crowd. 'They all look the same, don't they?' he would say. The student nuns also had a room reserved for them, but their door was always closed.

We had to settle for Hall's café, a tiny place on the corner of Leeson Street and Earlsfort Terrace. Here we could get a cup of bad coffee and a Woodbine cigarette for fourpence. During term time the customers were mainly students, but a few local residents would occasionally call into Hall's. During my early days in UCD, it was the favourite place for morning break by a small band of junior architecture students and I usually joined them.

For one period in those early years, it was about 1947/48, the most exotic visiting local was Jack Doyle, known as 'the Gorgeous Gael'. His early career was as a spectacularly successful boxer, but he was discovered to have a particularly dulcet tenor voice. He went on to Hollywood where he was less successful as a minor actor, but his gradual decline began with his short-lived second marriage to the voluptuous Mexican film star Movita. This was a real scandal in Ireland at the time, where the puritanical mores of the Catholic Church dominated everyday life. We were somewhat in awe of Jack Doyle. He was six feet, five inches tall, and despite his obvious downfall into alcoholism and near poverty, had more than a trace of his old arrogance and menace. He usually wore a long black coat which seemed expensively stylish but was now downright shabby.

I could earn a little more money in those poverty-stricken university days in a way that was almost exclusively the gift of architecture students. There was a multiplicity of college clubs and societies: drama, debating, political, sporting, archaeological, Irish language, poetry, book society, music, cinema and almost any subject that engaged youthful imagination. These groups all needed publicity for their activities, and the most effective and immediate showcase for this in the college environment was the poster. The architects had the tools and skills for this. One of the half-imperial sheets of cartridge paper, usually reserved for the prosaic Saturday morning building construction detail, could be discreetly switched for cartoons in a blaze of poster paint colours to ensnare new members or expectant audiences. The usual payment for each poster was a half-crown (two shillings and sixpence). A few of us became adept at producing the most enticing work and we were fully engaged. The more gaudy and riotous colours the better, but care had to be taken not to stray over into the risqué or what could be considered incitement to undermine college discipline. The university authorities would not tolerate that, and the banning of unsuitable or undesirable material was immediate. Irish youth had to be protected.

There was a definite sense of foreboding near the end of our first year with the looming inevitability of exam time. The high spirits, joking and occasional breaking into song gradually diminished in the first-year studio. It had, for me at least, been the most enjoyable period of my life. The rigid timetables of Synge Street, the autocracy, the hectoring and, above all, the sound of the leather-slapping echoing around the schoolyard were all in the past. I loved the freedom of the studio and being able to spend all day drawing and being introduced to design. However, for those of us who felt that we were liberated, a distinct and special species perhaps, the dread of actual exams became a gloomy reality.

The single most important and essential element in the exam assessment was the Year's Work, the portfolio of drawings and design projects. Failure in this meant not only not advancing to the next year, but the devastating prospect of a repeat of every studio project.

The exams are over. Our studio teachers have vanished; they are all part-time anyway and have probably gone back to their more lucrative jobs. The professor, always a nebulous figure, was nowhere to be seen. His shiny, lime green Armstrong Siddeley was no longer in its usual shady space. Our studio was locked and we, as junior students, felt cut adrift, wandering aimlessly from college to park and from park to college, unless we had money to sit in Hall's café.

The day finally arrived. A notice, posted in the college's entrance hall, stated that the results of the first-year examination in Architecture would be announced on such and such a date and time and that we should assemble in the hall. There were over forty of us, an unusually subdued bunch, gathered on that late morning in the college's bleak and anonymous entrance hall. There was a definite air of apprehension, and separate groups were forming. There were those who knew full well that they would fail their portfolio of the Year's Work, and the inevitable and grim prospect that awaited them. Even those of us who were fairly certain that we had performed well in most of our studio projects felt nervous about the seemingly myriad lecture subjects that had to be passed. We all dreaded the History of Architecture exam. Our bible was a textbook, *A History of Architecture* by Banister Fletcher, because the subject was taught in the most uninspiring manner: for junior students it seemed to be all about statistics and dates. We all feared any question on Gothic architecture, and when a major question on that period turned up on the first year exam paper, we all knew that we were possibly doomed. The glorious world of art and architecture, the history of civilization itself, to me at least, would be revealed in only a few short years, with my first trip to continental Europe.

A lone figure started down the wide staircase on the right-hand side of the entrance hall. He was wearing a black gown, clumsily thrown over his shoulders. 'He must be an academic,' we said. We had never seen him before. He had a clipboard in his hand and halted about five steps from the bottom of the stairs.

This was it, we thought, and crowded around below him. In a loud voice he announced, 'Here are the results of the first year examination in Architecture. All of the following are eligible to proceed to the second year of the course.'

He swiftly read out a list of names. It was arranged alpha-betically so I had to wait, almost afraid to breathe, until there it was: 'Sean Rothery'. I was through! The academic stepped down to the hall level and marched over to the bank of glass-fronted noticeboards fixed to the rear wall. He unlocked a door and fixed the sheet of names on the board, locked the door and quickly disappeared. There was no communication, no response to a clamour of queries.

We rushed to the notice and jostled to check that our names were actually there. Those whose names were not called out and not printed on the list looked confused, dismayed and even devastated. The call was, 'Did I pass the year's work and just fail some of the subjects?' Those who knew that they had failed their portfolio were resigned to the bleak prospect of re-peating the entire year or, for some, that it would be hopeless to continue on the course. It wasn't a very long list of names:

not many more than half the class went through. More would certainly follow us fortunate ones into the second year after the autumn repeat of various subjects.

Everyone began to move away from the noticeboard and distinct groups were now forming. Those of us who had passed were elated, but mostly greatly relieved and had gathered together. The talk was all about 'Where do we go to celebrate?' Some said 'Hartigans', the pub around the corner on Leeson Street. This was met with instant approval. However, many of those whose names had not ben called gradually drifted away.

I took one last look back into the hall as our jubilant group started to pour out into Earlsfort Terrace. There was a lone figure still standing at the noticeboard. I seem to remember that his first name was Joe and that he had rarely been successful in any of his studio projects. He was standing very close to the board, and I saw him suddenly breathing onto the glass and then rubbing it with his hand. Was he checking to see if his name was actually on the list? At once I had a vision of the unhappy face of Blacky in St Mary's primary school, and felt a wave of pity for Joe, standing there, alone and friendless. In truth, however, maybe my real emotion was a huge relief that it was not me who had been left alone.

I have sometimes asked myself if it was only relief that I felt in not being a loner, and even a failure, then how could those visions have stayed in my memory for so long? There was surely sympathy, knowing that, perhaps, deep down, there was a buried sense of insecurity in me, something that I would always have to confront and try to overcome.

Some of us, however, felt anger at a system that just called out the successful names on that short list, with no explanation for those left out. It was cruel and uncaring. It would have been so much more merciful to take aside those who had not passed their portfolio and advise them of their best prospects for their future. To condemn them to the shock and even shame of being left off the list, and for them to have to stand there in the midst of the exhilarated, successful students, was unpardonable. In my own future career as a teacher I made every effort to prepare, well in advance, those who were not going to pass, and thus save them from suddenly finding themselves the losers, mingled with the happy band who were heading off to celebrate.

My mother decided that I should have a room of my own, now that I was a university student. My father played no part in this decision – he was too busy at his various enterprises – but I knew they were both proud of my achievement. No other member of their own families had ever gone to even second-level schooling.

The hours spent in the studio were never enough to complete our design projects. The problem for me was getting my drawing board home each day from college. It was possible to transport the large and unwieldy double elephant board on the bus because, early on, we had devised simple wire handles, clamped under the board for easy carrying. My transport most days was by motorbike, so a different solution was needed. I solved this by a simple set of leather straps, along one side and over the rear wheel to secure the precious cargo. A windy day could be a big worry but, after a few frights, I learned to anticipate potentially hazardous situations and avoid a tumble.

The only space available in our small house was the 'front room'. We always called it that; a more posh term would be the 'parlour'. It was my mother's special space, reserved for the entertainment of visitors but otherwise sacrosanct. This room became my home for the next five years. It was a very pleasant space; in retrospect, possibly the best room in the house. The window, facing east, gave a magnificent view out to Dublin Bay, enfolded by the great whaleback of Howth Head. At night, with the curtains open, I could see the metronomic sweep of the light from the ancient lighthouse, the Baily, on the tip of the Head, reflected in the waters of the bay. On foggy nights the mournful wail of the foghorn sounded as far inland as Woodside. On a clear day in early summer, sunrise over the Irish Sea lifted my spirits and invigorated me for whatever tasks lay ahead. There was a front door, up three steps from the driveway, giving access to a minuscule hall. The floor consisted of small ceramic tiles, several of which were always loose and they were never replaced. We rarely used this entrance.

The selection of furniture was made in a manner that can only be described as haphazard. A huge and useless sideboard dominated one wall. I could never identify the wood – maybe a type of mahogany – but it was gaudy and shiny and it took a while before I could ignore its brazen presence. The top was far too high and narrow for me to prop up my drawing board on it. The cupboards were not suitable for storing my rolled-up drawings or to spread fresh paper out flat. The drawers, at least, could hold pencils, pens, inks, watercolours, set squares and all my various drawing implements.

In complete contrast, a little glass-fronted cabinet stood beside that monstrous sideboard. It was a delicate design with thin black framing that allowed a clear view of the cabinet's contents. The main display was a dainty tea set, a wedding present that was seldom taken out. Souvenirs from various trips were treasured objects, but my mother seemed most proud of the little models, mostly tiny ships, that I had made and these had a prominent place. The cabinet was her pride and joy.

There was, however, one significant feature of the room that I could not ignore and that was the carpet. It was shabby, dark and gloomy, a vile mix of colours from deep crimson to sickly yellow and with a violent floral pattern.

I arrived home one evening after a long day in the studio to find the room transformed. The hideous carpet was gone. In its place there was a luxurious carpet in a light shade of green, a lovely plain shade that made the room look larger and uncluttered. It was another of my father's successful auction bids. The venerable Canon Kelly of Sandyford Church had died and the contents of the parochial house had gone up for auction. The carpet was old and well-worn, but it was obviously a superior make and it looked magnificent.

A large, leather-covered sofa occupied most of the rear wall. I could prop my drawing board here at a suitable angle while I worked in comfort, sitting on a low stool. A shallow recess beside the fireplace had built-in bookshelves. My father had bought a complete set of an ancient encyclopaedia. This took up one whole shelf, leaving the rest free for my own meagre but growing book collection. Banister Fletcher's *A History of Architecture* had pride of place. This voluminous tome was a mandatory purchase and essential reading for junior students. My own copy was second-hand, dog-eared and tatty. I had bought it from a senior student, the usual method of purchase by impecunious juniors. It cost the enormous sum of ten shillings, four times my weekly allowance. I still have my copy.

The other compulsory, but less-loved, volume was *Architectural Building Construction* and it was, as the title page announced, by Walter R. Jaggard and Francis E. Drury. Its subtitle was *A Text Book for the Architectural and Building Student,* and our class had the very latest edition, hot off the press in 1945. The unpopularity of Jaggard and Drury was more because the textbook was associated with our Saturday morning class, Building Construction Detail. We were required to complete a half-imperial sized sheet of cartridge paper detailing, for instance, an up and down sash window; ledged, braced and battened doors; king post roof trusses; and, my favourite, fireplaces according to Count Rumford principles. These all had to be produced for our portfolio of Year's Work.

The fireplace on the fourth wall at home had a large cast iron surround. It was in a simple, even delicate, classical design. The high mantelshelf formed a cornice, while the surround was framed with a frieze and architraves in an egg and dart moulding. The centre panel had an embossed design, a decorative bowl, framed by floral, entwined garlands.

My own surround at the time was an incubating bubble of modernism, so I ought to have been eager to reject such relics, but I found it easy to tolerate and even to love the old-fashioned and quite feminine fireplace. The School of Architecture was on the cusp of change at that time. The powerful, classical influence of Rudolf Maximilian Butler may have been over. The new professor, J.V. Downes, was a definite modernist but the legacy of the old professor lived on, at least in our first year's immersion in the artistry of the Classical Orders of Architecture.

At night the sofa became my bed. The 'front room' became my room. I could now be alone for hours. I was in heaven.

That summer, after my exam success, I landed my first job as an architect. I thought I knew it all and that it was only a matter of time before I would be free to design my supreme great work. Such was my hubris after just one year's study. My self-elevation was demoted after a few weeks in the real world of work. I met the architect Desmond FitzGerald at his office in 6 Merrion Square on my initial morning. He greeted me warmly and announced that he had spent several summers in my grandmother's house in Woodside. What an amazing coincidence, I thought naively. It was many years later that I realised that there must have been a phone call from my father that had secured me the job, rather than my obvious potential for greatness as a designer. It did not take long in the ground floor of that office for the reality of an architect's working life to sink in.

The beautiful Georgian front room, facing the lush greenery of Merrion Square, was the practice's drawing office, while the rear room was the private domain of the 'boss', as we called him. Miss Smith was the secretary, and it was soon obvious to me that she was the person who was really in charge of the whole enterprise. She was petite, with prematurely greying hair and she had the sunniest personality. Miss Smith had a wry sense of humour, a steely, if well hidden, self-confidence and she knew how to handle the boss. There were two assistant architects in the office at the time, so the practice was quite a small one. I have forgotten the name of one of them. He was there for only a short time anyway, but I do recall that he was studying for a postgraduate qualification in town planning. The other member of staff was Fanahan Lyons, an experienced architect and, as I soon discovered, a highly creative designer.

Desmond FitzGerald was well known to us junior students as the architect of the newly opened airport terminal at Collinstown in north County Dublin. Photographs of this stunning piece of modern architecture were just being published in newspapers and journals. Wartime censorship had delayed any publicity about the building until the war's end.

Fitzer, as we also called him – but not to his face, as Doreen Smith warned us with a smile – was a tall and somewhat gangly figure. He talked explosively fast, to such an extent that his instructions were often incomprehensible. Fanahan frequently had to tell me what it was that he meant. He was notorious, I later found out, for his erratic driving and his eccentric parking. He was known occasionally to continue through a red traffic light. One morning I saw him in Ballsbridge avoid a red light and swerve around the signal by driving on the pavement. He would park his car anywhere and as close to the office as possible. Car parking was not much of a problem in those days.

My very first task involved me in the design of the new airport building; this engagement, however, could not be considered even remotely orthodox. I was directed to draw up a sketch design for a proposed new factory in the midlands, I think it was to be sited in County Carlow. A simple layout was all that was required, just a large rectangle with a line of windows down one side and a roof of steel trusses and corrugated sheets. The only embellishment and design innovation was that one end of the rectangle would have a small upper floor, actually a sort of balcony for offices. FitzGerald told me that a special staircase should give access to this floor. He went back to his office and then emerged with an enormous bundle of large drawings, bound together. The initial sheet was entitled 'New Airport at Collinstown'. In his usual impatient rush, he leafed through the sheets until he came to a floor plan that contained an elegant concrete staircase.

'Trace this,' he said, pointing to the staircase, 'and add it to the factory plan.'

This seemed to me to be a strange way to design and not very creative, but I did as I was told. I completed my sketch design for the factory with what I hoped would be a cheerful and artistic perspective drawing to soften the appearance of this dull and boring piece of non-architecture.

Decades later, when the Irish Architectural Archive was established, older architectural practices were persuaded to donate copies of their architectural drawings to add to an increasingly important collection of architectural documentary history in Ireland. I was asked to examine a large bundle of old drawings that had come from the defunct practice of Desmond FitzGerald. I turned up a perspective drawing where lush landscaping around an otherwise nondescript structure partially obscured its dullness. Exotic palm trees were arranged in clumps to enliven the scene.

'Have a look at this,' I remarked to a colleague, 'the tropics of Middle Ireland.' Then it dawned on me. The date on the drawing was 1947. The perspective was my work. I was into palm trees at that time in the first-year studio, where my palm trees were much in demand.

It did not take long for me to realise that the creative designer at No. 6 was Fanahan Lyons. I never saw the boss take more than a perfunctory part in the design process of any project. He always seemed to be in a hurry to be somewhere else while, in his absence, the conversation and banter in the office was invariably warm and far-ranging. It was a real education for me as an eighteen-year-old.

The most striking manifestation of the design talent of Fanahan came when the office won the commission for building the Moyne Institute in Trinity College. This would be a significant and rare modern addition to the fabric of the venerable university and, in fact, one of the first new major works of architecture in Dublin after the war.

The site for the new building was the southeast corner of the famous cricket ground. Fanahan's first sketch design for this new science building was of a white, delicately detailed modern structure, very much influenced by the Stockholm City Hall. The Swedish building was world-famous in the 1920s and was illustrated widely in architectural and building journals. Its architect, Ragnar Östberg, had given a lecture in Dublin in 1926. When the final sketch design was completed, a professional model-maker made an architectural model. It was fixed to a revolving base and covered by a Perspex dome. When this was unveiled and submitted to the clients and sponsors of the science institute, the design was greatly admired and praised. Then, inevitably, the moneymen took charge and the design was brutally eviscerated. Gone was the beautiful open colonnade fronting the Nassau Street façade, the open spaces filled in for extra laboratories. Almost every other elegant, inventive and even romantic feature of the original design was omitted. What was left was a run-of-the-mill, anonymous block: a sad episode and a lost opportunity to add a worthy piece of contemporary architecture to the sublimity of the Trinity campus.

I don't remember Desmond FitzGerald being even remotely concerned about this emasculation of a potentially landmark piece of architecture, but Fanahan Lyons was devastated and bitter about the final result. I had a small part in the design of the Moyne Institute but, after the debacle of savage cuts, could never claim credit for my contribution, even though this was untouched and remained from the original drawings.

I think that FitzGerald must have recognised my growing skill with a surveying level, honed in the UCD Archaeological

Society; hence his giving me the task of site layout for the new building. The main component of this was a contoured plan of a sloped grassy bank, on top of which sat the building. The bank was curved to form an appropriate corner to the cricket ground. My contoured bank may have survived the cuts, but the building is best forgotten.

I spent three months of my first year's summer job in 6 Merrion Square. I learned a lot, particularly about the less glamorous part of an architect's work. As a junior, I was probably shielded from the immense responsibility that an experienced designer would have for an actual building to emerge from the two-dimensional drawings. Just the same, I designed and completed working drawings for a small house in Killiney. To my delight, it was actually built some time later. At the end of September the boss presented me with thirty shillings. It may not have been a great salary for three months' work, but many first-year architectural students had to work for nothing, that is, if they could get into an architect's office at all.

When I moved up to second year I was still in the same studio, but in the upper section of the large space and with, sadly for some, a much smaller group. It was there that I met Fred Maguire, a fellow student who had a profound influence on my future life. He had to repeat his second year, something I found hard to understand. Fred was a beautiful draughtsman, a skill essential for passing a design project, but he still must repeat his Year's Work. I recognised him early on as a loner, but a very different personality from those lonely souls I had encountered in my formative schooldays. I could feel sympathy for them but, ultimately, I was profoundly glad that I was not one of them. Strongly armoured in his own individuality, Fred remained resolutely, even fiercely, his own master. He was certainly taciturn, sometimes to the point of long silences, but his own brand of wry humour would break out in a joke, or in a smile that invited a warm contact.

Fred casually mentioned one day about the recent formation of the Irish Mountaineering Club. I was instantly excited by this news and badgered him for more details. Two ex-Indian Army veterans, Joss Lynam and Bill Perrot, had returned to Ireland after the war. Seemingly they had been spared from protracted military duties and had managed to spend a lot of their time climbing in the Himalayas. They were both Irish so, when demobbed, they returned to reclaim their previous jobs. Joss was a civil engineer and Bill a quantity surveyor. Most importantly for me, the newly formed club promoted rock-climbing as well as general mountaineering. This new sport fascinated me and I was eager to get involved. Fred, too, had a motorbike and one Sunday morning the two of us set out to Luggala in County Wicklow.

From the high mountain road the lake was inky black and the great brooding cliff, sliced by rocky gullies and topped by darkly menacing overhangs, glowered above the waters. I couldn't wait to see for myself the pioneers of this new sport in action. Fred and I scrambled up the huge boulder field at the foot of the cliff, until the small team of climbers came into view. They were attempting to complete one of the first new routes to be forged up that granite face. The route was named Pine Tree Buttress, a series of steep slabs on the left-hand side of the main cliff. I settled down on one of the boulders to watch the progress above. It was apparent that rock-climbing was a slow and deliberate process with only one climber moving at a time, the rope being used for protection. It all seemed so calm and relaxed: lots of time sitting on little ledges in the sunshine, gazing down at the tranquil lake far below. I didn't attempt to climb that day but made a firm resolve that this was the future sport for me.

I had lived since childhood on the lower slopes of Three Rock Mountain and to climb higher was always my desire, a compulsion even. Somehow, my horizons always lifted and widened in every sense when I could climb up to my private nook, or scramble to the tops of one of the three huge granite rocks on the summit. Up there I would plan a future adventure or some exciting journey, or mostly just dream.

I remember my first real mountaineering expedition. I had decided to climb the Sugarloaf in County Wicklow with my younger brothers when I was about twelve. We borrowed my mother's clothesline, without telling her of course, because mountaineers used ropes for the ascent of formidable peaks. The Sugarloaf, soaring over the village of Kilmacanogue, seemed a serious challenge to us. We hid our bikes under a hedge and set out to climb the North Face. I had been reading about the intrepid feats of Victorian climbers in the Alps. I told my brothers that a rope was an essential safety device used by experienced mountain climbers. They believed my story. At least I think they did. The climb was a great success and we smuggled my mother's clothesline back without incident.

It was a seminal moment for me when I joined the Irish Mountaineering Club in 1948, but particularly for my friend-ship with Fred Maguire. My first climb was on the beautiful Twin Buttress of Camaderry, above Glendalough. In contrast to the crags of Luggala, this cliff high above the ancient miners' track faced south. The sun-warmed granite was a joy to touch and the very texture of the rock inspired confidence when one was attempting a difficult climb. I also met André Kopczynski there. Kop, although a close friend of Fred, was the opposite of him, an extrovert – handsome, bearded, dashing and with a devil-may-care attitude to life. He was another of those war veterans in university on a government grant and now a science student. Kop belonged to that extraordinary company of Polish young men who had escaped from the brutal occupation of their homeland by the Nazi invaders, and then went on to fight against them. André's job was to drive a supply truck through the valley below Monte Cassino during that prolonged and terrible battle in central Italy during 1944, having to endure day-after-day of murderous artillery fire from the heights above.

Having survived that maelstrom, I am sure that the airy sport of rock-climbing and alpine ascents would have been pleasant relaxations for him. As I discovered later, however, André had a wild streak in him. Fred was, essentially, an observer of life and found wry amusement in his own way. This could get him into trouble with those in authority as, for instance, in his career in the architectural studio. His drawing for the sketch design project 'A Monument to a Fallen Soldier' was signed by 'Who Tripped Him'. The joke, not appreciated by the teachers, cost him marks for his design.

A subsequent prank may have cost him his studio career. After completing another drawing for a sketch design project, he added a set of tiny, bare footprints in black ink, meticulously drawn, as if a diminutive figure had made a meandering path across the paper.

One of the earliest Irish Mountaineering Club annual dinners was held in the old Leenane Hotel in the west of Ireland. It was perfectly sited for the club's celebrations, situated on the side of the beautiful Killary fiord and surrounded by the great looming massif of Mweelrea mountain to the north and the wild wilderness of the Maumturks to the south. The nearby

Glen Inagh was the venue for the gathering. A campsite was set up close to the roadway through the glen on the banks of a stream that flowed across a wide stretch of flat bogland. The immense, darkly dominating cliff below Ben Corr was our climbing objective, only barely explored for rock-climbing.

On our first evening André Kopczynski and two other kindred spirits set off on a mysterious quest. The trio returned many hours later with a large fresh salmon, poached, they said with glee, from a private fishing pool which was attached to one of the posh Connemara hotels. They told us, in particularly high spirits, that a local man had taken them to an illicit whiskey distillery in the mountains. He had given them a bottle of poteen. It was a riotous party in the campsite that night. Kop entertained us with stories of his past and not much climbing was achieved the next morning. Fred Maguire just sat there with his habitual half-smile. He was the quiet one of the pair, but was a rebel at heart and enjoyed his friendship with the wild and ebullient Pole.

High summer and the club had its annual climbing meet to Ireland's Eye, an islet with two great rock stacks just off the coast of Howth and within easy reach of Dublin. A local boatman took our now growing band of rock-climbing enthusiasts out from Howth Harbour. That lovely warm summer's day was highly satisfying and most of the long-established routes on both the Inner and Outer Stacks were climbed. We had all enjoyed the easy and leisurely exercise on the sunny side of the stacks and it was time to leave. Our group was about to embark on the homeward boat when somebody said, 'Where's Fred?'

Nobody had noticed that he had wandered off on his own: not unusual for him and something that we all accepted, but this was different. He knew about the departure time and ignoring that was just not in his nature. None of us had been on the north side of the Inner Stack that day. There were few easy routes there, and the dark, sometimes slippery rock was usually ignored in favour of the sheer sensual pleasure of gliding up the warm dry routes and resting on the sunny ledges.

'That's where he must have gone,' somebody said, and a small party of us scrambled around the side of the stack and carefully climbed down to the sea level. We soon found Fred, upside down and wedged between two boulders. He was unconscious and, more seriously, his head was only a few feet above the surface of the water. Fortunately, it was almost dead calm, but the tide was coming in and soon could have drowned him.

One member rushed off to call for help but it was imperative to get Fred's body out of his perilous situation. We realised that he might have more serious injuries after his fall, but we had to move him. He was not very tightly wedged and we managed to ease him into a horizontal position well above the water's edge. We sat back and anxiously waited for a rescue boat, figuring then that Fred had obviously attempted a possible new route on the stack and had slipped and fallen. He had ignored the accepted rule of climbing at the time: 'Don't climb alone and with no protection.' Safety helmets had yet to be invented.

Our boat-man had sent up a flare. After what seemed an interminable wait, but was in fact less than an hour, the lifeboat came surging around the Outer Stack and manoeuvered right up to the rocky edge. Fred was expertly and carefully placed on board and was swiftly bourne to a waiting ambulance on the pier in Howth.

He recovered fairly quickly in hospital, telling us that he had wanted to solo climb a new route. This was so typical of Fred, knowing full well the attitude of experts to solo efforts. He smiled in his usual way when he said that he couldn't remember falling but just waking up in a hospital bed. He and André had planned their first alpine trip later that summer, and after only six weeks for his recovery from the fall, he felt he was fit enough to go.

They were two of the best climbers in the club at the time and their choice of venue was Chamonix in the French Alps. The savage silhouettes of the great rock needles called the Aiguilles dominated the alpine village. On their first day, the two friends started up the Nantillons glacier, intending to climb a regular and not too difficult route. Some way up the easy slope of the glacier, which was well covered with hard-packed snow, Fred slipped and slid down the incline, falling into a shallow crevasse. The mountain rescue team was called and swiftly arrived to retrieve Fred's body. He had been killed instantly.

It was the first climbing fatality in the club and a hugely sobering moment for those of us who had so joyfully embraced the new sport. We could only speculate why Fred had died because the fall, actually just a slide, was not a serious one. It was only six weeks, however, since he had been concussed in the fall on Ireland's Eye and maybe it was just too soon for him to attempt an alpine peak.

The following summer André Kopczynski teamed up with Peter Kenny and Frank Winder for another climbing season on the formidable Aiguilles of Chamonix. It was so typical of Kop that Fred's death had not deterred him from continuing in the sport that he had embraced with élan. I, however, knew that he was deeply saddened by the loss of his best friend. Peter, Frank and André, all newly graduated scientists, were the top climbers in Ireland at the time and an expert team.

After a successful ascent of one of the Aiguilles, called the Peigne, it was time to descend. The usual method of descent from these great rock needles was to abseil down, a method that was straightforward, swift and generally quite safe. In those days, before highly specialised climbing equipment was professionally designed and manufactured, anchoring the abseil rope first involved searching for a suitable knob of rock. A short loop of rope would then be placed around it, and the abseil rope threaded through for the descent. The rope loop or belay was then left in place. After many uses of the belay, it could have multiple loops, because each team added its own section of rope. This would be a prudent practice as older loops, particularly if they were of hemp, might have frayed or rotted. Sometimes, when many rope loops had to be used for belays in a long descent, climbers would be reluctant to cut small sections off their climbing rope to make a new loop. It was tempting to risk using a cluster of old loops, after checking to see if they looked sound. Every climber was aware in those days of the danger of this practice and dire warnings were given not to use old loops, but always to place a fresh one over the others.

Some way down from the summit and after several easy and safe abseils, the trio arrived at a place where there was a large bunch of loops already in place. These looked quite safe and they agreed not to sacrifice any more of the climbing rope for yet another loop. André volunteered to go last, then the first two slid down to the next resting ledge without incident. When André started and swung out to descend, the combined old loops parted and he fell straight down to the others. He died on that high mountain ledge during the night.

It was about a year to the day since his friend and climbing partner Fred Maguire had died, only a short distance away, on an adjoining glacier. The news filtering back home shocked us all, but for me it was a double blow. These men were giants to me, although they were only a few years older than I was. André was buried near Fred in the Chamonix cemetery, a tranquil place below the savage peaks, shining snowfields and the frozen ice rivers of the Glacier des Bossons. It was a fitting final place for these two friends, surrounded by the graves of generations of mountain climbers.

Meeting Fred and André changed my life. Their sudden deaths could have turned me away from the mountain world that was increasingly becoming my passion, but I learned the lesson of caution from their mistakes. It was André's impetuosity that killed him, while Fred's death was more enigmatic. He always had that steely determination to go his own way, no matter what the consequences might be.

André Kopczynski was, in many ways, like my father. He loved life, could never resist a challenge or risking a new adventure. Wariness would never be a part of his nature. I could, when I got to know him, enjoy those aspects of the dashing Pole, but in subsequent years I would reject the same traits in my father. As a result, caution became firmly fixed in my nature.

Fred Maguire was in many respects a rebel. I admired this trait of his and sometimes envied it. He had contempt for authority, even though this could cost him dearly in the despotic regime of UCD at that time. He never told me why he had to leave the course in the School of Architecture. Fred went to work for a firm that supplied steelwork for building contracts. His job was banal: a draughtsman who produced endlessly repetitious drawings for the steel reinforcement of concrete. His early death on the high mountains that he loved so much was, perhaps, a better end for him. I always thought that Fred would never have endured a life bereft of imagination.

The rebel in me remained dormant in my student years. This was largely because I hugely enjoyed my five years in the School of Architecture. I loved drawing and most days in the studio were invariably a joy. I even managed to get satisfaction at least, if not pleasure, from the Saturday morning Building Construction Detail class. Most architectural students hated this task, or maybe it was just seen as spoiling the weekend. I became quite an expert on Count Rumford's Fireplace Principles and also on the complexity of having to fit multiple flues into one tall chimneystack. This expertise would have been of great value to me if I were living in the eighteenth century but not much use thereafter.

There was sheer sensual pleasure, however, in brushing watercolours across the lightly textured surface of Whatman paper, when finishing a design drawing. Standing back to admire the result was the highlight of the studio experience. I cannot say that our teachers had any great effect on our work, with the possible exception of Willie Maguire. His contributions were appreciated by us all in both the second and third year of the course. I always felt that we were mostly educated by osmosis. Daily life in the studio may have often been one of cheerful banter, but we also walked around and shared our work with others, and above all were immersed each day in a creative atmosphere. Sharing ideas and in particular offering advice was usually gratefully accepted, but if someone was in imminent danger of embarking on a potentially disastrous drawing decision, we would swiftly advise caution. On occasion, however, we could be too late or, on a well-meaning rescue attempt, advice was rejected and inevitably a calamity would result.

One morning, on a casual stroll around the first-year studio, I saw a student starting to draw two parallel lines, forming a sort of border all around her completed work. Not a great idea, I thought, but I didn't say anything. She was one of a small number of students who never asked for advice. Some time later, with a couple of fellow first years, we saw to our horror that she was filling in the space between the double-lined border in black indian ink. She was applying this with a scratchy pen and it was a painfully slow process. It was too late for us to offer any comment or to advise caution. When she had finally completed the filling in of the border, she stood back to view the result. It had converted a quite reasonable design drawing into a grossly inflated, funereal, giant mourning card. Sadly, she was one of the many casualties in that brutal announcement of first-year results and we never saw her again.

The university had only a pitiful collection of architectural books, but the main sources of inspiration for us were the bound volumes of a few well-known architectural journals. The most memorable of these was the German monthly *Moderne Bauformen*. Up to about 1934 this well-known journal was filled with superb photographs of the new, white, sleek buildings now appearing in some parts of Europe. When the Nazi regime took control in Germany in the mid-1930s, everything changed. This modern architecture and its cognate modern art were banned as communist and degenerate. In its place a new architecture of the Third Reich was ruthlessly imposed. The manifestation of this diktat was an oppressive, overbearing and crudely unrefined Neo-Classicism. For the new domestic architecture of Nazism there was to be a return to the vernacular of the German Alps: heavy wooden balconies and steep roofs with massive stone plinths and chimney-stacks. The editors of the journal, however, although obeying the new order, found a way to still show illustrations of new and exciting modern architecture. Sweden and Switzerland were showing the way forward and these were the buildings that architectural students were eager to see. Fortunately for the editors of *Moderne Bauformen,* the regime did not interfere with displaying this exciting architecture from these two neutral countries.

There were a few volumes of a curious American journal called *Pencil Points.* It was of little interest to us fiercely dedicated disciples of Modern Architecture. The buildings illustrated were mostly folksy, timber-framed and in the traditional styles favoured by a vast swathe of American states. What attracted me, however, were the beautiful pencil drawings copiously displayed in each monthly issue. I was already, since boyhood, drawing with a pencil in sketchbooks, but there was a verve and lushness about these American artworks. Soft pencils were used to give tonal variations in free drawing. This was a refreshing respite from the more formal ink line work, a necessity for architectural projects. The sensory feeling of line drawings could be mostly mechanical, but soft pencils would caress in the most sensual manner the textured cartridge paper. A wide variety of tones could be achieved by leaning heavily on the pencil to produce a smoky black, with gentle stroking for the lightest shade.

It must have been in third year that I had my one and only brush with authority. It was a small studio at one end of the gallery and still under the same old glazed roof that covered the first and second year's large studio. One morning in winter there were only three of us working there when it began to snow. Some of the glass panes in the roof were cracked or broken and flakes of snow had started to fall onto our drawing boards. We made jokes about this but soon began to think about protecting our work. We knew that there was plenty of timber and other materials left over from previous Rag Day constructions in the semi-basement workshops, and after a foraging trip we came back with the makings of temporary shelters. We may have had less daylight on our work but our drawings were protected and, of course, we thought that our ingenuity would to be praised.

The professor was seldom seen up there in the old studios but someone must have ratted on us. We were severely censured for vandalising college property. We had to remove the shelters immediately and were suspended from the studio for three days. Later generations of architectural students in schools worldwide would have the design and construction of temporary shelters as a regular project. The reaction was a typical one of the regime in the college of that era, and came shortly after the university president, Michael Tierney, banned the college annual Rag Day.

I don't remember much about my first Rag Day in UCD, except that it was a disorganised affair, although I enjoyed the experience of flouting authority for a whole day. The theme was loosely based on the war in Palestine and a number of students who had motorbikes decided to dress up as Palestine police. The plan was to take over policing duties on O'Connell Bridge. There was a famous garda who did point duty in those days at the junction of Burgh Quay and Westmoreland Street. He was tall and thin and moved with a balletic grace, particularly when wearing long white gloves, and he gave sweeping hand signals. When a couple of us arrived at his station on our motor bikes, dressed, as we thought, in the uniforms of the Palestine police, he good-humouredly handed over point duty to us for a short while.

Dubliners were quite tolerant of students' Rag Day at that time. They were seen as a fun few hours for the city, and a goodly sum of money was always collected for various charities. The university authorities were, however, not so tolerant, and strict rules were generally imposed on organisers before permission was reluctantly and grudgingly given.

It was my second and last Rag Day that was the most memorable. The parade through the city was usually the highlight of what was recognised as a student carnival at the start of the term. A fellow student, Jack O'Keeffe, proposed that we produce a theatrical presentation for our contribution which would proclaim the creativity of the School of Architecture. Jack suggested making Ancient Egypt the theme of the display and he spent hours in the workshop building the centrepiece of our exhibit: Cleopatra's royal riverboat. He begged, borrowed and otherwise acquired the materials and, although he had a good deal of help, the bulk of the work was Jack's. His studio attendance suffered and, instead of being awarded credit for his energy and creativity, I'm sure his portfolio-marking suffered. The vessel that emerged from the UCD workshop on the eve of the parade could not be passed off as a true replica of an ancient Egyptian riverboat, but in our eyes it looked great.

A third-year student volunteered to be Cleopatra. He was short and of slight build, clad in a white chiffon robe, and when he reclined on a chaise longue – actually a broken old sofa – he made for a highly passable and seductive Egyptian queen. He, or rather she, had two female slaves waving fronds over her while a band of male slaves pulled the boat, now on bicycle wheels. The remaining architecture students were dressed as toga-wearing Roman soldiers, with plumed helmets and wooden swords. We were by far the best display in an otherwise raucous, disorderly but highly enjoyable day of high jinks. On our return journey over O'Connell Bridge, our float was suddenly attacked by a group of engineering students, who unceremoniously dumped Cleopatra and her slaves out of the boat, which was then tilted up, pushed over the parapet and toppled into the Liffey. For a moment it floated serenely down the river but swiftly sank and we watched weeks of loving labour lost for ever. 'Typical of those bloody engineers' was the rueful comment. 'Philistines.'

I'm sure that it wasn't just this incident that caused all future Rag Days to be banned, but it possibly contributed to the death of the one and only day when the student body could, with impunity, be naughty. Jack O'Keeffe never said where he got the idea of Cleopatra's boat. The famous films of Antony and Cleopatra came to Dublin in later years, but there was one earlier film entitled *Cleopatra*, made in the late 1930s and featuring the smouldering Claudette Colbert in the eponymous role.

John Charles McQuaid, the archbishop of Dublin from 1940, would have condemned utterly any depictions of a sultry Cleopatra as extremely dangerous to the morality of Irish men, particularly to us vulnerable students. A writer, Gabriel Fallon, spoke of the dangers of cinema-going to what he called 'The Unsophisticated'. He went on to say that 'the influence of the cinema is, on the whole, tending towards moral, artistic and intellectual degradation'.

We did, however, on our few afternoons off work, flock to the magnificent Theatre Royal to enjoy the high-kicking dancers, the Royalettes, and whatever film the Censorship Board had allowed to be screened.

It wasn't just the evils of sexual indulgence that Irish men and women had to be protected from, although the Catholic Church considered this to be the gravest sin. It was also the pervasive influence of communism. America was gripped in the post-war years with paranoia about the rise of communism throughout the world. This reached its peak in the early

1950s with the show trials of McCarthyism and obsession with this 'ungodly' ideology spreading to the vulnerable shores of Ireland. One of the early battles to protect the morality of the native flock was the proposed performance of Arthur Miller's play *Death of a Salesman*, first performed in the United States in 1949. A virulent campaign by Catholic organisations was mounted to prevent its first Irish performance in the Gaiety Theatre in Dublin. The production was to be by the famous theatrical duo, Micheál Mac Liammóir and his partner Hilton Edwards. Irish militant Catholic groups denounced the play as a 'hotbed of communism'. They claimed as their source for this charge prominent and mainline US Catholic publications.

The queue for the first night stretched from the doors of the theatre all the way to the top of Grafton Street and beyond. I was with my friends Aidan and Bernard, accompanied by their girlfriends. Fortunately, we had arrived early to get in line, but were still a long way from the entrance. The queue grew rapidly behind us as a large cohort of protesters began marching up and down, waving placards and shouting about godless communism and haranguing the theatregoers to boycott the play. We did not see a single person leave the line and the reaction that the zealous protesters were getting seemed to vary from completely ignoring the clamour to outright amusement at their antics.

We managed to secure seats and the theatre quickly filled to capacity. Just before the curtain was raised, Micheál Mac Liammóir appeared, and from the front of the stage expressed, in his wonderfully mellifluous voice, a warm thanks to the protestors outside for the superb publicity they were giving to the first Dublin performance of the play. He was hugely applauded and *Death of a Salesman* was a great success.

It was hard to see how the overwhelming pathos of Willy Loman's story could be considered a 'hotbed of communism'. Here was a man bewildered that he was being abandoned, while sure that he was still 'well liked'. It was revealed later that the communist calumny was just that: a careful omission of one word from the initial American condemnation. It had stated that 'some plays were hotbeds of communist ideology backstage and this – *Death of a Salesman* – is one'. By the sly dropping of the single word 'backstage', a singularly sad and moral story by a master playwright was denounced. It was only a small affair, however, in an era of obscurantism in Ireland, with the wholesale and vicious banning of books, many by Irish writers, and the prudish censorship of films.

The most extreme of the militant Catholic groups at the time was Maria Duce. Founded in 1945 by Father Denis Fahey, it was openly anti-protestant, anti-semitic as well as anti-communist. Censorship of the theatre was only one of its many truculent demands. I was in my final school year when the organisation was founded and I heard about it from one of the senior pupils who had been trying to recruit youth members.

On one occasion he attempted to persuade a group of us in our final year to join in what he called a crusade. 'Our motto is,' he said, 'a punch in the face for Christ.'

'Whose face?' we asked.

'Any enemy of the Catholic faith. Yours, if necessary,' he said.

He was laughed at, and certainly got no encouragement from the school authorities. I saw him later at one of Maria Duce's vociferous protests. Archbishop McQuaid tolerated Maria Duce for a period; after all, he undoubtedly shared many of its core aims and beliefs. However, he never gave them his official imprimatur and eventually, wary of their extremism, did not go so far as to call for the body to disband but, instead, he instructed the organisers to change its name. It remained in a different and less vocal form until the early 1960s.

I first read William Hazlitt's *Essays* after being introduced to the writings of great English essayists in Tommy O'Rourke's sixth-year class in Synge Street Secondary School. In Hazlitt's essay 'On the Pleasure of Painting', I was entranced by one lovely sentence: 'From the moment that you take up the pencil, and look Nature in the face, you are at peace with your own heart.'

It was, however, Hazlitt's 'On Going a Journey' that inspired me and rekindled a desire that I had always had, since those boyhood explorations on Three Rock Mountain. I resolved that one day I would go on a journey. Hazlitt's opening sentences of his essay made an immediate impression:

> One of the pleasantest things in the world is going a journey; but I like to go by myself. I can enjoy society in a room; but out of doors, nature is company enough for me. I am then never less alone than when alone.... I cannot see the wit of walking and talking at the same time. When I am in the country, I wish to vegetate like the country. I am not for criticizing hedge-rows and black cattle. I go out of town in order to forget the town and all that is in it. There are those who for this purpose go to watering-places, and carry the metropolis with them. I like more elbow-room, and fewer incumbrances. I like solitude, when I give myself up to it, for the sake of solitude.... The soul of a journey is liberty, perfect liberty, to think, feel, do, just as one pleases. We go on a journey chiefly to be free of all impediments and of all inconveniences; to leave ourselves behind....

The sentiments of liberty, solitude and, above all, the idea of never being less alone than when alone, particularly appealed to me. When I first read it, the somewhat arcane language of the essay was a delight. I wanted to pack a rucksack and just go on a journey.

Travel to continental Europe was impossible during the war and difficult for several years after the conflict ceased in 1945. I finished third year in the School of Architecture in 1949, when constraints on foreign travel eased, although there were still severe currency restrictions in place. I began planning to make my first long distance-journey before entering the fifth and final year of the course.

The Vatican decried 1950 to be a Jubilee Year and pilgrimages to Rome were encouraged throughout the Roman Catholic world. The year was enthusiastically welcomed in Ireland, where it became named as Holy Year. Travel agents were now able to offer organised tours to Rome, thus making it easy and relatively inexpensive to undertake the long journey. In the early years after the war air travel was only for the wealthy, and tours by coach or train were the usual options for would-be pilgrims.

Here was my journey: long distance, and with that essential element for me, a clear and elysian destination. I had no intention of joining any official tour of Rome as a pilgrim. My journey had to be a solitary one, close to nature and above all to provide a challenge. The prospect of navigating my way across Britain and then along the length of France, over the Swiss Alps and finally down the spine of Italy was daunting. Planning the trip was highly seductive, however, and I could not wait to get started. There was one big problem and that was the time to be allotted to the adventure: 1950 was the start of my final and thesis year in the School of Architecture and this commenced in mid-October of that year. I also needed to earn some money that summer, before setting out on my journey. The time I would have available was from late August through September, returning home in early October. My plan was to travel to Rome and back by bicycle.

It was still only 1949, however, and there was still the fourth year of the course to face, but I was confident that I would progress as smoothly as I had done so far. A far greater question was that I had not undertaken a long journey up to now, and particularly one by bicycle. In addition, I had never travelled beyond Ireland. Five years of world war had left me, and others of my generation, in a cocoon of isolation.

I decided to make a long journey in Ireland in the autumn of 1949. My friends from schooldays, Bernard and Aidan, had planned a holiday on Achill Island in the far west of Ireland and I joined them. After a week in this splendid place with them, I would set off and attempt to cycle around the top half of the country and back to Dublin. By this undertaking I would have tested not only the machine and other practical elements, but above all myself. Would I have the endurance and the sheer tenacity to complete the marathon journey?

The three of us took the train from Dublin to Westport one morning in mid-September, our bicycles stored in the guard's van. It was a glorious ride across the causeway on to the great island of Achill, where the landscape was dramatically differ-ent from the lushness of the Mallaranny woods we had just left behind. The scattered and unplanned village of Keel was where we would be based. My developing belief in the new gospel of Modern Architecture should have made me disapprove of this wilful and brazen display of individuality. There was no order whatsoever in that haphazard settlement. There was, however, a beautiful harmony in the random spread of identical white-washed walls and gables, each capped by black-tarred and slated roofs. The dramatic scene was dominated by the blue-black mass of Croaghaun, a Paul Henry landscape come to life.

The week on Achill passed quickly. It was my first time in the far west and the majesty of that wild spectacle was over-powering. The long white sands of Keel beach stretched to the brooding Menawn cliffs. The great storm beach of rounded stones reared up like a massive berm, sheltering the wide grassy *machair* to the rear. Each deep green-blue Atlantic roller broke into sparkling surf, endlessly repeating the slow march to the sands. The rocky berm, however, told a different story – of terrifying winter storms, with enormous waves breaking into spray as they smashed over the great barrier.

One morning we cycled up the rough track towards Keem strand but soon had to abandon our bikes and continue on foot. At the top of the steep hill we paused and looked down to the fresh view opening up below. Unlike Keel beach, which was wide open to the full force of the Atlantic, Keem was tucked away, embraced and sheltered on three sides by steep hilly slopes. The sea was the deepest blue and the sun shone on the white sands. The prospect was sublime.

A different spectacle, however, unfolded when we reached the strand. We had heard about the nascent shark-fishing in-dustry on Achill and here was evidence of what that entailed. The green sward above the beach was littered with the detritus of the new activity. Several crudely built sheds were being con-structed, for bunkhouses we were told, and nets and ropes were spread out on the grassy slopes. The tide-washed sands were still pristine, however, and the three currachs neatly upended above the highwater mark were reassuringly emblematic of the west of Ireland that artists embraced.

The place was deserted when we arrived, except for one fisherman repairing nets. He told us about the new industry and was highly enthusiastic about it. Basking sharks were huge, he told us, many even longer than one of the currachs below. These great fish were killed for their oil, which was extracted and could yield a handsome profit. It was a godsend for Achill, he said, and we could not disagree. There was a dark side to the enterprise, however, and a much more unpleasant one than just the ugliness of litter. The method of killing these great fish, sometimes in huge numbers, was repellent in the extreme. Nets were spread out from one headland, and when a shark was caught, the fishing crew would race out in a currach to stab the creature with home-made spears. Blood from the slaughter would spread out over the clear, clean water and often end up as a stain on that beautiful white sandy shore.

Croaghaun towered over the beach and I just had to climb it. I set out alone. The sheer slope made for a strenuous ascent but I revelled in the experience. The steepness ended suddenly and the spectacle was sensational. From the summit the ground fell away in a stupendous cliff, two thousand feet down to the ocean. I sat and felt overwhelmed by the majesty of the vision. Only the slender, rocky finger of Achill Head stretched out beyond the precipice, a feature that was endlessly eroded and sculptured by the monstrous power of Atlantic storms.

My week in Achill passed quickly. I was eager, impetuous even, to start my long homeward journey. I said goodbye to my two friends, they still had another week of holiday and then, back to their jobs, while I was still a student, free as a bird. Those were my thoughts on that early morning as I started out from Keel. The sun was shining, puffy white clouds in a blue sky; with the wind behind me, my mood was euphoric. I was sure that I would succeed. It was an exhilarating ride on that long, largely flat road all the way to the causeway bridge and the mainland. I turned north here and followed the coast road, past a maze of meandering inlets of the calmest of waters. The tide was low for most of my cycle up to the beginning of the great wilderness of Nephin, and the shores were largely strewn with enormous tangles of seaweed.

I pedalled up that lonely road for hour after hour, and gradually the elation I had at the start of the journey ebbed away. I began to realise two things. The first, and one that I savagely acknowledged, was that the bike was a disaster for this venture. It was far too heavy, even without the two panniers strapped over the real wheel. It only had one speed, and was going to cause me endless distress before journey's end. That is, if I ever reached the end. The second revelation was that the trip was going to be much harder than I had lightly dismissed beforehand. Such was my gloomy mood when I eventually arrived at my first night's stay. With casual optimism, I had planned to keep a detailed and daily diary of the adventure, but I was so exhausted that evening I didn't write a single word.

I have only fleeting memories of that journey north. It was the wind: a relentless buffeting that stretched my endurance to the limit. The long, almost treeless sections of road are best forgotten, but when I finally turned east that cruel blast was now behind me. My spirits rose and I thankfully ended my second day on the road a lot less doubtful about the way ahead. My limbs were stiff, however, as was my rear end, sorely chaffed after hours on the saddle. An Óige youth hostels were somewhat primitive in those days. Hot water was seen as a luxury and hot showers would have been considered sinful pleasures. Suffering was necessary and morally sound for those who desired to embrace the great outdoors.

I washed in cold water, deciding that it was sure to be good for me, fell into my bunk bed and slept for eight hours.

My route north would take me close to Drumcliff churchyard and the grave of William Butler Yeats. The poet had died in 1939 in the south of France, where he had been buried. He had expressed a wish that his last resting place would be in the graveyard below the cliffs of Ben Bulben in County Sligo, but the war made that impossible. Finally, in 1948 the Irish government arranged to have his remains exhumed and ceremoniously transported back to Sligo Bay by the Irish Navy. Yeats was reinterred close to the simple but elegant Church of Ireland building at Drumcliff. It was in Tommy O'Rourke's English class in Synge Street that I was introduced to the Yeats's poetry, the early poems especially. I saw the newsreel of that reinternment that had taken place only just over a year before, and I now wanted to see for myself where he lay.

The slender shaft of the early Christian High Cross seemed a fitting signpost for Yeats's last resting place, whose myriad lyrical words sang of Ireland. I walked the short distance from the roadway to a peaceful place. The plain headstone bore the words of the epitaph he wrote for himself:

Cast a cold eye
On Life, on Death.
Horseman, pass by.

Tall trees surrounded the little church, with the long escarpment of Ben Bulben a dominant backdrop. I stood for a while, remembering the words of some of the early poems, so loved by my inspirational English teacher, especially those of Sligo:

Where the wandering water gushes
From the hills above Glen-Car....

He stood among a crowd at Drumahair;
His heart hung all upon a silken dress....

The wind has bundled up the clouds high over Knocknarea,
And thrown the thunder on the stones for all that
   Maeve can say.

Tommy O'Rourke's favourite was 'The Lake Isle of Innisfree' and the words of the second verse came back to me as I stared out from this tranquil place:

And I shall have some peace there, for peace comes
   dropping slow,
Dropping from the veils of the morning to where the cricket
   sings....

The sonorous beat of those lines, and many more, would stay with me for a lifetime.

The road north from Drumcliff has some clear memories for me. Before setting out from my lodgings, I checked my map to plan the day's journey. A long sliver of scimitar-shaped beach that reached out from Streedagh Point intrigued me. A substantial lagoon separated this impressive landscape feature from the main shoreline. The place was only a short distance from my route, and I felt it was such a tantalising formation that it just had to be explored. A rough track led from the little village of Grange, eventually a wide and undulating sweep of well-cropped grass gave way to sandy dunes. I dumped my bike, scrambled to the top of the rise and looked down to the great beach. I was at one end of what seemed like miles of yellow sand, curving away to a distant rocky headland. The strand was wide open to the ocean and, even though it was an almost calm day, a succession of waves broke into sparkling surf, which died away only on the pull of the sand. A storm beach of well-rounded stones reared up and protected a superb panorama of rolling, green-grassed dunes.

I started to walk towards that distant headland. It was if I was alone in the world. The feeling was one of elation and, like Hazlitt on his journey across a lone heath, I also wanted to laugh, run, leap and sing for joy.

Clambering over the rocks at the beach end, I turned the corner and saw a tiny cove. It was sheltered by the headland that revealed itself to be a grass-topped islet at high tide, separated from the shore by a jumble of large seaweed-covered boulders. The sand, unlike the main beach, was a pristine white and lapped by slow wavelets. The sun shone and to swim was almost mandatory. The water was like glass, so clear that each pebble and shell was visible below the surface. I waded out to where I could plunge into a deeper sea, and after the initial shock of the cold, luxuriated in the voluptuous pleasure of the water's embrace. After the swim, I climbed up to one of the dunes above the sand and, finding a grassy fold, sheltered from the breeze, spread out my towel to sunbathe.

It was just like the nook on the mountain above my home in Woodside. The prospect before me was divine. Across the vast expanse of cerulean ocean, the hazy blue mass of Slieve League and the mountains of south Donegal filled the horizon. I dozed there until late in the afternoon and began to think that this was nirvana.

I roused myself from my lazy reverie and knew that it was too late for me to continue my journey north. Walking back along the beach, I decided that my only option was to return to my previous night's lodging and start again the next morning. I had mixed thoughts on that walk. My steely determination to complete this hard task, come-what-may, was surely challenged by the way I had given in to such a day of sheer sensuality. I would make up for it the next day, I resolved. I would do a double stage.

Looking back at the sparkling seascape, my final thought was: who cares? It was a day of shameless indulgence and I had loved it.

I have no memory about my onward journey, after that blissful day at Streedagh. I may have made that promised two stages in one go; I certainly needed to make up time, and know that I did not travel out to Slieve League. The western coast of County Donegal had been carved by the Atlantic Ocean into an intricacy of inlets, bays, headlands, peninsulas, promontories, dozens of sandy beaches and the mighty cliffs of Slieve League. The coast road was, therefore, a long meandering route that snaked around every obstacle and would have taken me days to travel. I took the easiest option, which was straight up the east of the county. My goal was the youth hostel at Downies, on the Rosguill peninsula, far out on the county's deeply serrated north coast.

At some elevated point on the road out from the village of Carrikart, I had my first sight of the great beach of Trá na Rossan. It was an achingly beautiful scene, with the setting sun about to dip below the distant horizon. The tide was out and the great sweep of shining sand mirrored the evening sky. The beach faced south and, unlike Streedagh or Keel beaches, was more sheltered from the might of the Atlantic.

The hostel, perched on a high point of the peninsula, was a former holiday house, built in the late nineteenth century, in an Arts and Crafts style. It had been generously donated to An Óige in the 1930s. I was the only guest. The warden told me that I would probably be the last, because he was soon closing the hostel for the winter. Next morning I made up a lunch, filled my flask with tea and set out to walk the length of the beach to the farthest point south. It was a glorious morning of sunshine and, with that sharp clarity of colours that is so typical of early autumn, I had never felt so alive. The tide was fully out and an immense, perfectly smooth, sandy plain was spread out before me – an almost boundless prospect.

After what seemed like hours, an outcrop of black rocks loomed up, signalling an abrupt change in the beach's direction. I paused here, and on a sudden impulse stripped naked and ran out to the sparkling ocean. I waded through shallow surf until just beyond the last breaker where I could swim out into deeper water. Here I floated languidly on the slow, greeny-blue rollers. It was elemental, even hedonistic; I have never felt more a part of nature.

On the way back I sat for a while on a low bank of marram grass and thought about the past days. Why am I doing this journey? I asked myself. It was so hard, the only consolation being these two wonderful beach days. The rest of the time was mostly suffering; endless pedalling on a bicycle that I was tempted to jettison and hitchhike home. I was lucky with the weather, except for the constant wind. There was little rain. That evening in the hostel, yet another solitary one for me, I came to a decision. Letterkenny, a day's ride away, would be my turning point. I would have two options there. I could turn north and continue all the way around the coast and finally south, back to Dublin, or I could give up the struggle, admit that I had had enough and head southeast across the middle of the country and straight home. It would take me three days I thought.

The next morning was dull with a hint of rain. I cycled away from the Rosguill peninsula in a mood that matched the weather: gloomy and increasingly resigned to abandon the journey. My thoughts along the way were about failure and what it meant for the really great adventure I had planned for the following year. If I found it so hard to complete this far shorter journey, how on earth could I cycle to Rome and back? I was also feeling lonely. It was all very well to agree with Hazlitt on the virtues and indeed the pleasures of being alone, but I had not had a proper conversation with anybody since leaving Achill and I longed to meet fellow adventurers.

After a few hours it began to rain, compounding my misery at the prospect of failure. On a high point of the road there was a hand-painted sign that said 'Hostel', with an arrow pointing down a boreen to a little inlet from the sea. To hell with this, I said to myself. I can't go on and it's back home for me by the shortest route tomorrow.

The road had a grass strip in the middle and led down from the slopes above to a narrow ravine. Lush holly and hazel bushes filled the sides, the hazels were thick with nuts and many of these were ripe. I filled my pockets and there was the hostel. It was perched just above the water and was open. I came in to find two people in the common room. They were a young couple from Belfast, Heather and John. They had been walking and hitch-hiking in County Donegal and were now on their way home. There was an immediate rapport between us. They were keen mountaineers, although not serious rock-climbers, and we found that we had much in common. We stayed up late that night, sharing stories of our joyful outdoor adventures in our young lives, especially the sheer ecstasy of wild swimming.

The next morning after breakfast I told my two new friends that I was proposing to abandon my planned long trip around the north of the country. I also shared with them that this was to be a test for a greater project next year, and now I wondered about my ability to complete that long cycle after failing in a far shorter journey. Deep down, however, I was already re-energised after the previous night's high-spirited sharing of our mutual stories. I secretly wanted encouragement to stick to my original plan. Heather and John's immediate response was, 'You can't give up; we'll be continuing around the coast, staying at hostels along the way, why not join us and meet each evening?' It was just what I wanted to hear. My torpor of the day before had vanished. I felt rejuvenated and bursting to go on.

I walked up the boreen with my two friends, wheeling the bicycle. When we reached the main road, I left the couple to walk on until they could thumb a lift, while I continued with renewed energy towards Letterkenny and the decisive junction. We had arranged to meet at a hostel not far from the city of Derry which was not too great a distance for a day's cycle. Shortly after I had left them, a horn beeped behind me and as the car swept by, the two waved and shouted, 'See you later'.

My lighter mood continued for a long time, even after I turned north at that key junction. I have only fleeting memories of the rest of the long way around the north coast. I was so buoyed up by the prospect of meeting up with Heather and John each evening that I don't remember any of the hardship. We three swam on a late afternoon from one of the magnificent sandy beaches on that coast. It was now early October, the water was warm after the summer and the beach was deserted. Our last hostel together was near the Giant's Causeway. After we had scrambled down to view this extraordinary geological wonder, we sat to view the sunset on a hilltop high above. John and Heather were now anxious to head home, but said that I must come and stay with them on my way back south. I was sad to part company with them the next morning, but looked forward to visiting their home in two days' time.

The verdant Glens of Antrim were a complete contrast to the untamed and savage beauty of the west and the road south now hugged the coast all the way to Belfast. It was an exhilarating ride for a long way, but as I got closer and closer to the big city, it was no longer enjoyable. I was tired, the traffic was noisy and I wanted the ordeal to end. Traversing the city, I made my way out to Hollywood and was relieved to easily find Heather and John's house.

The luxuries of a hot bath and a soft bed were sybaritic delights after the Spartan world of youth hostels. I stayed on with my friends for a further day and evening. It was a slow, peaceful time for me but also a time for reflection. What had I proved so far? The answers to myself were mixed. I had cycled most of the way around the top half of the country, so that was an achievement. Another voice remembered the travails, even times of outright misery. I had to accept the reality. I was exhausted and did not want to go on. I decided to contact my father.

We did not have a telephone at home, so I called him at his garage in Stillorgan. He congratulated me for my efforts, but something of the level of jadedness must have come across in my voice, particularly when I said that I was not looking forward to cycling the long road from the border.

'That's a terrible road to cycle,' he agreed. 'I could drive up to the border and pick you and the bike up,' he said. 'How would that be?'

I didn't need much persuasion. With an early start, I thought I could easily cycle the direct route from Belfast to the border, just outside Newry, in a day. We fixed a time in the late afternoon and I ended the call with huge relief. Mixed with this sense of elation, however, I had a niggling thought that I was abdicating too easily from the task I had set for myself. I looked at my map and saw that I could take the road down one side of Strangford Lough and then the coast road by the Mourne Mountains and reach Newry by Carlingford Lough. This would be an enticing route to take, close to the Irish Sea and then the majestic Mournes. It would most certainly be a fitting end to my journey. I was good at rationalising and could now banish all thought of failure.

This route, however, would take me two days. I rang my father back and told him my fresh idea. He said that it sounds like a good plan and we agreed a new time to meet. It would be like old days with my father, when we went on trips together. This was my thought after our talk. I went to bed that night happy.

I said farewell to Heather and John the next morning and we agreed that we must meet again. It was an easy cycle down the side of Strangford Lough and soon the bulk of Slieve Donard filled the horizon. My destination for the night was the youth hostel at Bloody Bridge. I had been there before. In the winter of 1946 I had persuaded a fellow first-year architecture student to hitch-hike with me up to the Mourne Mountains. I had been intrigued by the story of the Brandy Pad, an eighteenth-century smugglers' route through the mountains. This led from a landing place near Bloody Bridge, and then via a rough path to the far west side of the range. We did this trek during the Christmas break from college from west to east; youth hostels near both the start and the finish of the smugglers' path made a one-day's journey possible. The hostel at Bloody Bridge was welcoming. I was eighteen, at the end of my first journey.

I cycled away from the hostel on a different morning, now two years later. I was also elated that my new journey was ending. The Mournes looked different from that winter's scene. Each mountain was etched sharply in the sunshine of early autumn; their names sang of Ireland – Slieve Bearnagh, Slieve Lamagan, Slieve Binnian. The colours were luminous: purple heather on the slopes above the yellow blossoming October furze, or whins, as these was known in the north of the island. The road south ran close to the sea, glittering blue in the morning light, until it turned inland before opening up to the shores of Carlingford Lough. On the other side of the lough the long ridge of Carlingford Mountain enfolded the beautiful wide waterway, until it was compressed into the aptly named Narrow Water. A gentle cycle along the lovely Newry River and at last I could cross over to the southern bank. It was a short ride to the border but I was too early for the time I had agreed to meet my father. I dawdled along, luxuriating in the thought of the imminent end of pedalling.

I was now quite satisfied that the border was my journey's end. The 'Customs Ahead' sign appeared and I wheeled my bike slowly past the hut on the northern side, with only an indifferent glance from the officer in charge. The same indifference greeted me at the southern post and there was my father's car, parked close to the Border. He was early and my relief that my suffering was over was palpable. Our normal greetings would be usually perfunctory but this time the greeting was a little warmer. However, our habitual reticence conversing together prevailed. The bike was placed on the roof of the Ford. My father was never concerned about scratches or dents; cars were workhorses for him. Ropes held the machine in place, tightened over the front and rear bumpers, and we were off.

I have no memory of that car journey home. I'm sure I must have slept, but I do know that I was intensely grateful to my father for my deliverance. I asked myself, some time later, what lessons had I learned from the experience of that journey, which was intended as a test for the greater adventure to come. The first was, of course, that the bicycle was useless and had to be replaced. The second and possibly the most serious lesson was the stark reality that even such a short trip was much harder than I had anticipated. Would I have the steely resolve to make that journey to Rome and back? I invariably and blithely ignored the fact that Rome would only be halfway. The great journey was nearly a year away, however, and such thoughts, worries or doubts could be put aside, for a while at least.

I have little memory of my fourth year in the school, except that the old cosy studio on the gallery, with the makeshift partitions, was no more. We had a new studio, specially laid out for us superior seniors, as we thought ourselves to be. It was in the semi-basement of the main building facing Earlsfort Terrace. It did, however, have a somewhat insalubrious entrance through the anteroom for the men's toilets. I remembered that Flaubert wrote somewhere, 'Architects always forget to put in the stairs.' Were the authorities that gave us the new studio reminding us not to forget the lavatories?

My first passport was issued on 2 August 1950. The information was in three languages, Irish, English and French. There was a personal description table and in it I was noted as a student, born in Dublin, 5' 9" tall, brown hair and with an oval face. There was no section in the personal table for sex. A matching table beside the first was headed 'Wife'. Similarly with the facing page, which had two spaces for photographs. The first space was entitled 'Photograph of Bearer' and this had my grinning face, definitely oval in shape. The matching space alongside was entitled 'Photograph of Wife'. Was there an assumption in those days that the bearer would always be male and would have a wife in due course? Was there instead a more innocent or less calculated assumption that when a man and woman got married it would be more economical to have both on the same passport? When I found my old passport, many decades later, my first reaction was that the format would be more applicable to Saudi Arabia.

The next page stated, in three languages, and in capital letters:

THIS PASSPORT IS GOOD FOR THE FOLLOWING
COUNTRIES
All European Countries, their Possessions and
Territories Overseas, Turkey, Syria, Lebanon,
Egypt, Cyrenaica, Tripolitania, French North
Africa, Spanish Zone of Morocco, Tangier

There were strict currency regulations in those immediate post-war years. I distinctly remember that I was restricted to a maximum of £20 for my travelling expenses, and this was entered in my passport. I was constantly reminded of the limit on my long trip.

I bought a new bicycle. It was a sports model, much lighter than my old one and so smart-looking that my spirits rose and I was now ready for my really long and epic journey. It was a Hercules Kestrel model, and was entered in my passport as such. I had been saving money for the great trip for some time; pay from Desmond FitzGerald's office each summer was barely enough to cover my expenses but I found a way to earn a satisfactory sum to allow me to travel, if not in style, at least to survive. After my second year in college I rented a small section of turf bog, beside the bigger area that had been worked by my father up to the last years of the war. There were a few weeks of perfect weather in June and July and, mostly at weekends, I cut enough turf to make a lorryload; drying winds and sunshine swiftly completed the work. I found a buyer, a relative of one of my fellow students. My father provided a lorry and driver and, after the delivery of the load to an address in Sandycove, I became richer than I had ever been.

I started my journey to Rome on 28 August 1950. I had already made the decision to take the train to London from Holyhead, so my actual bicycle journey would begin in the British capital. This could save me up to six days and make it possible to get back to college in time for my final year. I stood on the deck of the morning mail boat out from Dun Laoghaire harbour and watched the Wicklow and Dublin mountains fade away. It was not long before Snowdonia loomed up ahead. The Irish Sea on that lovely calm morning seemed more like a peaceful lake before we tied up on the quayside at Holyhead. It was a long train trip to London and after I had retrieved my new bicycle from the Guard's van, I set out to find my night's billet. This was to be in Clapham Deep, one of several underground air raid shelters built during the 1941 blitz and subsequent aerial bombardment. I had heard that this particular shelter was now being used as a hostel for impecunious travellers like myself. There were over 180 steps down to what was then one of the deepest series of tunnels dug for shelter during the war. When I had descended I was surprised by the orderly layout. It was well lit and provided with a long line of neatly laid out bunks. I was tired after a long day and slept like a baby.

The road to Brighton and on to Newhaven, where I would embark on the boat for France, was a far busier route than any I had encountered in Ireland. It was a good wide road, however, with a surprising number of people cycling. It was an easy ride and I passed the Royal Pavilion in Brighton, with only a perfunctory glance, mixed, as I recall, with the smugness of a committed Modernist, dismissing such architectural frivolities. Decades later I could only smile at those youthful certainties. I was standing, at that moment, in the Alhambra, spellbound at the sublimity of Moghul architecture and the tranquillity of the gardens.

I had a far different reaction, on the other hand, when the famous Brighton Pier came into view. Competing ideas had swirled around in my head for my thesis project in the coming final year. Looking at this long horizontal platform, balanced delicately on iron legs and stretching far out over the sea, I immediately resolved that the theme of my subject must be about the alliance of land and water.

It was only a short cycle to the port at Newhaven and I was soon on my way to what Hazlitt called 'the laughing shores of France'. When I landed in Dieppe and collected my bike, my first task was to buy food. Bread seemed to be the easiest option for my first foreign shopping experience. I eventually pointed and emerged with a delectable, freshly baked baguette. I couldn't wait to bite into the wonderfully smelling crust and I cycled away, satisfied that my first shopping had been successful. My route to Paris was southeast via the city of Rouen.

I suppose I should have been prepared for my first view of that city. As a schoolboy, I had kept up with all the news of the progress of the war, but the sight of the consequences of that conflict shocked me when I cycled into Rouen. Allied bombing had reduced the city to an appalling vista of ruin; even the famous Gothic cathedral was badly damaged, and the superb spire seemed perilously close to collapse. It was barely six years since the invasion forces had smashed their way up from the Normandy beaches, driving the German armies north.

The town was eerily deserted but the well-cleared streets, with neatly piled mountains of rubble alongside, spoke of a place ready for rebirth.

Paris was a revelation. After the devastation of Rouen, the great city was spectacularly normal. I cycled along quiet streets with no sign that huge armies had twice, in the past few years, passed through, yet had left the place unharmed. Hitler had ordered the retreating Germans to lay waste to the French capital but his generals, no doubt aware of their future reputations, riskily disobeyed his orders.

The road from Dieppe and Rouen led directly to the Arc de Triomphe where I cycled down the magnificent promenade of the Champs Élysées. I saw outlandishly ostentatious shops, chrome-framed windows with huge declamatory lettering overhead and, the ultimate exciting sight for me, exotic pavement cafés stretching all along the wide avenue. My immediate destination was a Camp Volant. These camps were set up just after the war to cater for some of the millions of refugees and displaced persons wandering over a ravaged continent. A number of the camps survived into more settled times as low-cost, short-term stays for indigent travellers, like myself, although, as I discovered later, there were still very many refugees looking for shelter, even five years after the fighting had ceased.

I found the camp after a few enquiries; it was on a small green space just behind the Champs Élysées. There were a few lines of sturdy-looking tents, with a larger kitchen/dining room marquee at one end. I checked in and was directed to one of the tents and my bunk bed. I was handed a shiny steel receptacle, which had differently shaped spaces scooped out to hold each meal item. This was an American army rations tray, an ingenious object, indestructible, easy to use and, most importantly, easy to clean.

Next morning I explored the quays along one side of the Seine. Bridges always fascinated me but nothing prepared me for the astonishing variety, beauty and sheer perfection of the bridges over that river. My first sight of Pont Alexandre III left me astonished. From downriver, the majestic sweep of the single elegant arch spanning the waterway took away my breath but, when I came onto the bridge, the exuberance and ornateness of the sculptured figures and decorative devices were almost too much for my new Modernist certainties to take in. Those certainties were severely shaken and I found myself marvelling at this display of architectural, engineering and sculptural delight.

The bridge was nearly deserted on that early morning, but when I turned from gazing at the river I saw the girl in the red dress. She was leaning over the opposite parapet. I remember that moment as if it was yesterday and the feelings I had then were overwhelming. I was in Paris, on this bridge where extravagance, folly and sensuality were all around me. I was twenty-two, unattached and still living at home, but now far away from an Ireland where such indulgent pleasures had no place in its narrow, pietistic and church-dominated society.

The girl walked away, briefly glancing across at me but then continuing on to the quay on the far side. To this day I wondered what might have been if I had the courage or brashness to speak to her. Apart altogether from my lack of French, I certainly could not afford to take her to a café and I doubt if she would have been impressed by a meal on an American ration tray back at the camp. I watched her stroll away, the red dress turning the corner, and the moment was soon over.

The Rodin Museum was nearby and open. Unlike many art works snatched from Paris galleries during the Occupation, the Nazis stole few of the works by the great sculptor. I was intrigued to see that the original of The Thinker, a plaster cast of this, one of the most famous of Rodin's works, was in the National College of Art in Dublin. The grubby, white plaster cast in Kildare Street was a shoddy copy of the brilliant original bronze. The other famous work was The Kiss. It was hard to imagine a replica of this celebration of sensual love being tolerated in the Dublin of the time. The huge Gates of Hell bronze was terrifying, and the story of Rodin's vast number of works was unimaginable. I wondered how could one man produce so much in a lifetime?

For my second and last day in Paris I travelled along the banks of the Seine to the Île de la Cité and my first sight of Nôtre Dame. I entered through a darkened vestibule into the nave and, as my eyes adjusted to the dimness of the light, the soaring space was spell-binding. I think that my epiphany happened at that moment. Memory of those dry-as-dust lectures on Gothic Architecture, coupled with the ponderous prose of Banister Fletcher, faded in the reality of being in that sublime place. I marvelled at the daring of the builders of these stupendous structures: such perfect marriages of engineering skill with architectural beauty. These men, often anonymous master masons and carpenters, could visualise in three dimensions and set out with such precision the great skeletons of stone. It was humbling to think that these giants of their craft were the forbears of my new profession.

When I first entered the cathedral I was alone in the vast nave, but after a while a small number of people filtered in, and most settled as a group. After a few moments I heard the great organ begin some tentative notes as if warming up and I wondered if a recital was about to take place. This was a highly exciting prospect and I found a seat near the group. As if on cue, the deep thunder of the bass pipes seemed to shake the whole structure and with the contrasting and high-pitched reed sounds I recognised the music of Bach. It was a blissful experience to sit there and be embraced by the wondrous sound.

When the music finally stopped and the group began to leave, the man beside me turned and spoke to me in French. I answered, with one of my few phrases, that I understood only a very little of the language. His English was a lot better than my French as he told me that the organist was the famous Marcel Dupré and that this had been just a rehearsal for a longer recital later in the week. I had heard the name of this organist and composer from my younger brother, Eamon, who passed on his early passion for classical music to me. My neighbour told me that Dupré was the resident organist for another Paris church, St. Sulpice. I thanked him and left in a haze of emotions; excitement certainly, but mostly a warm feeling that life was good and my journey ahead full of promise.

Early next morning I left Paris and headed southeast, now reinvigorated and eager to reach the border and Switzerland. Passing through the forest of Fontainebleau, a brief view opened up of the great Royal Palace. There was no time to visit, and anyway I had little enthusiasm for such a fussy and florid style. I have few memories of those long stretches of road. It seemed dreamlike to cycle for hours on level and straight sections where the traffic was at times light to non-existent. However, I do have one visual memory and that is of a road, lined on both sides with regularly spaced poplar trees that seemed to reach out to a far horizon. Looking at my atlas now, I remember the names of the towns I passed through, but have no visual recall of them: Troyes, Chamont, Langres, Vesoul went by until I reached the Belfort Gap. Here this wide opening between the Vosges Mountains and the Jura range revealed grim evidence of a world war battle, the first signs of war since Rouen. Rusty burnt-out tanks were dotted in the fields and ruined buildings had shell holes blasted through and window surrounds peppered with bullet marks.

I needed somewhere to stay that night but had no address of a hostel. I enquired in my halting French at a *boulangerie* where I bought bread, and a kindly baker directed me to a place nearby. The building looked shabby on the outside; obviously it was not an official hostel. The *gardien* looked at me dubiously, or so I thought, as I asked if I could stay for the night. After a few moments of my mangled French and his limited English, I realised that he didn't think that this place was suitable for me. I understood him to say that homeless men were often residents there. He also said that sailors discharged from ships in the Mediterranean regularly slept in the hostel, when making their way up to Rotterdam or Hamburg for another vessel. He advised me that if I decided to stay, I should stow my passport and money inside my sleeping bag for safety. I was too tired to worry about anything as he led me to a large dormitory. There were about twenty beds, simple iron-framed affairs, and the room looked clean and neatly kept. Only a few of the beds were occupied and, except for a cacophony of snores, grunts and groans, the night was peaceful and eventually I fell fast asleep. I washed in cold water in the early morning and thanked the *gardien* who directed me to a cheap café in the town for breakfast.

Later that day I crossed the frontier into Switzerland. It was a triumphant moment. I felt that my great journey was now well and truly progressing. Switzerland was another world. The sun was shining from an impossibly blue sky and everything looked so pristine, clean and prosperous. The cultivation of fields continued almost to the neatly mown road verges; ever inch seemed to be used. The houses were brightly painted and flowers decorated multitudes of house balconies. Everywhere else I had visited so far seemed, in contrast, drab and neglected.

Lake Lucerne, with its deep blue water and pleasure boats, was like a fantasy but the real drama was the great barrier of the Alps that dominated the view south. Green forested slopes rose abruptly from the flat plain and shining snowfields peeked out above the foothills. I was enchanted at the sight and there and then vowed to return soon to climb these superb mountains.

The first serious challenge was to cross over the St Gotthard Pass, one of the highest mountain passes in the Alps. I stayed the night in Andermatt, a village on the plain and the beginning of the road over the range and down into Italy. I started early, just after first light, and soon the enormity of the task ahead dawned. For the first hour's cycling the road seemed first to wander off more in a westerly direction than south, then, in a sudden hairpin bend, sweep off for ages in the opposite and more easterly direction. This looping went on and on: at this rate I wondered if I could possibly get to the top in one day? The hours went by and now I could appreciate the brilliant engineering marvel that the road designers had achieved. The great serpentine wandering of the route, sometimes stealing far into valleys in the mountain walls and then twisting, the road sneaked around the contours, relentlessly gaining height for hour after hour. Higher and higher the mountain landscape changed. I was now well above the tree line and the first patches of remaining winter snow speckled the slopes. Then I came into the first of the semi-tunnels that were covered by long reinforced concrete roofs. These spanned the road and were constructed to divert snow avalanches over the passage and down the steep slopes below. At the end of that long day, the summit of the pass appeared, and a sign that read 2,091 metres. I later calculated this figure to be almost 7,000 feet, about twice the height of Carrauntoohil, Ireland's highest mountain. Among the several buildings scattered about on the small plateau that formed the pass, there was a mountain hostel. I checked in and, not long after a meal, fell into my bunk and slept the night through.

A high alpine morning: a stillness that made the panorama of snow peaks a spectacle of wonder. I stood on a grassy mound and knew that I was destined to come back again and again for both adventure and solace in this high mountain world. There was a higher rocky knoll nearby, just an eminence perhaps, rather than an alpine summit. I just had to climb it, for it would be my first alpine peak, or so I could tell myself.

I still had that formidable road descent to make, all the way down to Italy, and was eager to start. From the very beginning the gradient was gentle and the freewheeling was exhilarating. I wanted to sing for joy as mile after mile went by effortlessly. It was down, down, down on seemingly endless sweeping curve after curve, interrupted only by an occasional hairpin bend. Breaking here was essential and I hoped my brakes would not burn up. After the first few of these more acute bends, I began to gain confidence in dealing with them. The hairpins were so cleverly designed that I could swoop around the bend while hardly slowing. On and on I spiralled down, until the first hamlet appeared far below. Above the chalets the road made an amazing, almost circular loop as if I could herald my arrival at this first habitation on the other side of the pass. The road then straightened, the gradient gradually became flatter, and the sign ITALIA appeared.

There was by now the usual currency check at the frontier, to satisfy the officials that I was not smuggling money, I presumed. My much-depleted wallet was all I had. Unlike my entry into both France and Switzerland, however, there was a handwritten note entered in my passport, next to my entry stamp, that I was entering Italy *con bicicletta*. I wondered did that mean that I would be checked on leaving the country that I still had the machine? What would happen if the bike were stolen? It didn't bear thinking about.

My mood changed after less than an hour on Italian roads. The elation from the swooping ride down from the pass had died away and I grew increasingly agitated by the erratic and sometimes reckless antics of Italian drivers. The road to Milan was narrow and there was far more traffic than I had encountered in France or Switzerland. I was not sure which was more frightening: traffic coming up behind me and blaring their horns or the sight of cars or trucks driving towards me and causing me to veer almost into roadside ditches. By the time I reached Milan I was drained, despondent and exhausted. I found a hostel, after a long and frustrating search, but following a meal and a good rest, I decided to make a new plan in the morning. Reluctant to start cycling again right away, I wandered around the centre of Milan in a state of indecision. I hardly glanced at the great Gothic Cathedral; my first impression was that it was ostentatious and florid. Decades later on a visit to Milan I marvelled at this sculptured masterpiece in stone. I was much more impressed at the time by the Galleria, an impressive shopping arcade with a high glass roof.

I found the railway station and asked the price of a ticket to Rome. It sounded quite cheap and, on an impulse, I bought a ticket that allowed me to stop off in Florence. I was immediately enlivened; the thought of days of enduring Italian traffic on the roads south to Rome had thoroughly depressed me. I had endured enough, I thought, and I wasn't a true pilgrim anyway, where suffering was an essential ingredient of the religious experience.

The train was packed to capacity; even the corridors were jammed. I had to stand all the way to Florence and, after re-claiming my bike from the guard's van, was vastly relieved to be squeezed out onto the sun-baked platform of that beautiful city.

The youth hostel was a cheerful and exotic place in a run-down building near the centre. The recreation room was on the first floor with a balcony looking out to a small courtyard. There was an outdoor cinema that night, with a big screen on an end gable wall. I settled down on the balcony with a couple of English-speaking hostellers to watch a John Wayne western. The film was voice-dubbed instead of our expected subtitles. When the hero appeared, his taciturn, almost monosyllabic drawl was translated into machine-gun Italian. We nearly fell off the balcony laughing. It was the most fun I'd had since leaving home.

I went out with my sketchbook next morning, determined to make a number of drawings, as I had done already in Paris and Switzerland. The Ponte Vecchio was my first destination. This medieval bridge had always fascinated me, but particu-larly its more recent history. Three segmental stone arches spanned the River Arno, while the bridge itself was lined with covered shops on either side of the carriageway. In 1944 the German armies, retreating north after the Allied invasion of the Italian mainland, destroyed all the bridges over the river with the sole exception of the Ponte Vecchio. Theories about this disobedience of Hitler's orders to lay waste all structures in the wake of any German retreat usually conclude that the German general in charge did not want his name to be forever known as the vandal who had destroyed this world-famous treasure.

Settling down on the eastern riverside, I contemplated my subject. I was first attracted to the elegance of the arches spanning the swiftly flowing Arno, as well as the treble-arched colonnade in the centre, but most of all I loved the sheer quirkiness of the scene. Shop owners, no doubt dissatisfied by their very narrow floor spaces, had added extensions over the waters, supported by rickety-looking timber struts. This gave the bridge an extraordinary character of richly chaotic beauty and was a perfect prospect for a drawing.

For a subject as intricate as this, I began slowly and carefully but soon became aware that I had a number of onlookers. I usually hate anybody watching me – it does not allow me to get immersed in the work – but I got an idea. I reached for my hat and surreptitiously added a few coins and then placed the hat behind where I was sitting. The drawing progressed well and I forgot about my audience, but when I had finished I discovered to my surprise that my coins were now augmented by a lot more lira. It wasn't a fortune but I was satisfied by my first efforts as a pavement artist. Later it dawned on me that I should have made several sketches of the bridge and sold them. It could have, for a while at least, halted my growing poverty.

The temporary bridges over the river were perfect objects for sketching: their essentially fragile and haphazardly rushed appearance was grim evidence of the recent devastating war. The Renaissance Pitti Palace was a different study, a regular architectural drawing, as was the one I made of Brunelleschi's great innovative dome for the Duomo. It was time, however, to move on. I was getting anxious about my timetable.

The train to Rome was as packed as the one from Milan. Standing room all the way once more. I left the central station, jubilant that I was finally in the ancient city and my journey's end. It was actually just halfway; I still had to return home, but concern about that task could be left aside for now. My first and immediate stop was the Vatican, where the registration office for pilgrims was located. When I cycled into the vast and splendid Bernini piazza, the signs for pilgrims pointed through the beautiful colonnades to a doorway marked JUBILAEUM MAXIMUM. I knew this was the sign for the Pope's Holy Year. It felt a little intimidating for me; would I have to prove that I was a genuine pilgrim? The room was large and crowded but the atmosphere peaceful. There were chairs for everybody and I sat down to observe what was happening. Announcements were made regularly, mostly in Italian, and a few people would amble up to one of a line of manned tables, laid out at one end of the room.

My apprehension grew as I sat there. I knew that the majority of the pilgrims from Ireland were groups, many church-organised and led by priests or even bishops. Would I be questioned to establish my authenticity? Would I have to produce a certificate from my parish priest or a holy medal perhaps? Was I poor enough? I was beginning to fear being exposed as a fraud and having to slink out in disgrace, with disapproving looks from the genuine assembled pilgrims.

A voice called out, 'Any English speakers?' I stood up and looked around. There was nobody else standing, so I walked up to the speaker's table and sat down.

A man smiled and said, 'Welcome to Rome. Where have you come from?'

'Ireland.'

'Excellent,' was his reply as he handed me a piece of paper. It gave me four days free board and lodgings in the city; all that I had hoped for. 'Will you be able to find that building?' he said.

I looked at the address. It was on the Via Aurelia. 'Certainly,' I replied, 'I have my bicycle.'

'Wonderful,' he said and stood up to shake my hand. It was as easy as that. I walked out, dizzy with joy.

I found the Via Aurelia but the first building number was a low one and my address appeared to be far out on that road. It didn't matter, and I sped along in high spirits. Rome was friendly to cyclists; there were dozens of us. My new lodgings were in an apartment block, obviously one of the many constructed during the rise of Mussolini. It was in the monumental fascist style favoured by that regime and by the Nazis but, unlike Hitler's new bombastic and crude Neo-Classicism, the long history of Italian art and architecture added a lightness and delicacy to the white buildings of the new estates.

Exploring Rome on a bicycle was the ideal method, except for the worry of having it stolen. Strangely, I have no memory whatsoever that this possibility bothered me. Was I naïve? I don't think so, but on reflection, since stealing bicycles was a common occurrence in those days of post-war Europe, maybe I was just lucky.

The Sistine Chapel had to be first on my list, and at a time before mass tourism engulfed almost every art and architecture treasure in the world, it was an overwhelming experience to be alone, staring up at the multitude of swirling figures on the fresco-painted ceiling. I wondered how on earth Michelangelo had painted it? Then there was the great dome of St Peter's: here was the painter and sculptor now turned architect and engineer.

After that Renaissance feast, it had to be ancient Rome. The Forum, the Coliseum, the Baths of Caracalla all went past in a whirlwind. Those dry History of Architecture lectures now came vividly to life. The star turn for me was the Pantheon. I stood spellbound under the great dome, looking up at the deeply coffered ceiling to the blinding light spilling from the oculus. The dome was almost 2,000 years old, constructed by the Romans in their innovative concrete and without our modern steel reinforcement. Any architect, young or old, could only have felt humbled in that divine space, and by the genius of the distant forbears of our profession.

My four days in Rome went by in sensations of wonderment, awe, animation, excitement. I gorged on the art but soon felt satiated. The prospect loomed of facing the long journey home with little or no money. My last evening in the lodgings felt like an anti-climax as I gloomily pondered my options. I couldn't face many more days cycling along Italian roads. I counted my remaining lira; there was just enough for the cheapest train fare to Genoa. I had addresses of several religious institutions and these were possibilities for a free bed and, with any luck, food. My optimism grew and I went to bed thinking that maybe all would be well.

The next morning I breakfasted well and then stuffed as much food as possible, mainly bread and fruit, into my panniers and set off for the central station, the Roma Termini. To my surprise I saw my first example, on the European mainland, of Modern Architecture. This was a sleek, steel and glass addition to the railway station, but the most enduring image for me was the incorporation of a preserved section of ancient stone wall into the fabric. This image would stay with me into my future life as an architect.

The train was again packed to the doors for most of the slow journey north. I have one memory of being harangued, in a jokey and quite friendly way, by two Italian men about what I understood to be the inevitability of the Communist Party ruling the world. My Italian was limited to a few phrases, as was their English, but they even tried a little Latin, which I did understand. It was all in fun anyway and they left in good humour at some stop along the way.

The train arrived in Genoa in the late evening and I cycled out to the first address I had of a religious institution. When I rang the bell at a somewhat anonymous doorway, it was opened by an individual who glared at me in the most hostile manner. I enquired if I could stay the night but was answered by a loud flood of Italian and the door slamming in my face. I suppose that I should have felt humiliated – after all I was a beggar – but I was actually stunned and really angry. I had never in the entire journey so far been treated with anything but cheerful kindness and a warm welcome.

Riding off down to the coastal road, I spotted a laneway leading down to a little beach that was barely visible in the fading light. I walked out on the sand to find a place behind a large boulder. I unrolled my sleeping bag and sat for a long time, leaning against the rock and gazing out over the sea. It was so peaceful that my annoyance died away, listening to wavelets whispering over pebbles at the water's edge. Bread and fruit washed down from my water bottle made for a satisfactory meal and I soon fell asleep.

Waking before dawn, I had a delectable swim in the warm Mediterranean. At first light I rode off, with renewed optimism that all would be well, despite the fact that I did not have a single lira left. It was an enjoyable cycle along that coastal road with the sparkling blue of the sea on one side and brooding mountains on the right. My next address was near the frontier with France, and when a church with a prominent bell tower appeared I saw that it was a monastery. A long avenue of pines led up to an iron gate. There was an old-fashioned bell with a rope attached and when I pulled it, a small figure dressed in a long brown robe came to the gate. He greeted me with a warm smile and immediately opened the gate and led me inside to a beautiful little garden. He didn't ask me anything but ushered me into the refectory where a few other monks and a group of three lay-dressed men were sitting. He pointed to a place on a long bench and gestured for me to take a seat.

I was served soup from a steaming tureen and a basket of crunchy bread was passed along. The talk was lively and all in Italian. I wolfed down the soup and bread, with the beaming smiles of my welcoming monk facing me across the table. At the end of the meal a monk brought me to a bed in a small cell that was spotlessly clean and neat: an iron bedstead with a wooden crucifix on the wall overhead, a spare cupboard and a little table. He left me and I lay down for an hour or so of calm reflection. After the previous night's experience, it renewed my faith in human nature. I must have dozed off when I heard the sound of singing from the oratory. It was that mesmeric sound of Gregorian chant that had haunted me in those far-off days as an altar boy in Sandyford church – seminarians from nearby Ballinteer occasionally sang at mass. I stole into the rear of that peaceful place and sat to listen to the beautiful and hypnotically repetitious phrases.

After the chanting was over, my new monk friend told me the time for the evening meal and showed me where I could wash and brush up. I could hardly believe that we would be eating again and thanked him gratefully. For me the evening meal was a feast and in true medieval monkish style we were served red wine. I nearly converted to a religious life on the spot.

The next morning, after a breakfast of a bowl of coffee and more crusty bread, I thanked my hosts for their wonderful hospitality, shook hands all around and set off on the dramatic coast road towards the frontier with France. At the Italian custom stop my bicycle was examined. I wondered what on earth for. They checked that the name and number of my bike in my passport matched those on the machine. Was it because I might have been involved in a sinister bicycle-switching fraud? The official sent me on. The French customs just waved me through and I sped off along a glorious road, eating up the miles past Monaco and Nice until I arrived into the beautiful resort of Cannes. At the Crédit Lyonnais I changed the remainder of my pounds (keeping back just one pound note) into French francs. I was acutely aware that it was a pathetically small sum that had to last me for the rest of the journey through France.

My destination was the Île Sainte Marguerite, a small island just off the seaside town of Cannes. I had heard that there was a recommended youth hostel here. I parted with a few of my precious francs for a boat that carried me out to a landing place near the massive Fort Royal. The hostel was in one of the many buildings inside the defensive fortifications of this former army barracks and prison which now was semi-derelict. When I checked in, I met a small group of French fellow hostellers who greeted me warmly. They were students from Marseille, spending a few days on the island. They told me about the Fort. I had not known that it was reputed to be the prison where the 'Man in the Iron Mask' had been incarcerated in the late seventeenth century under the orders of Louis XIV. I had read the Alexandre Dumas story of that famous and mysterious prisoner and was intrigued to find myself in his actual prison.

That evening the French party saw me rummaging on the kitchen shelves for some half-used packets of food and promptly asked me to join them for the evening meal. I accepted the offer with alacrity and, after the meal, spent the evening with them, swapping stories of hostelling adventures in a mixture of my bad French and their limited English. It didn't matter; we laughed and sometimes sang until it was time for bed.

In the morning my new friends invited me to join them for a swim. They had discovered a place just below the walls of the fort where the water was calm. Swimming naked in the warm Mediterranean was the most sensual experience and, as I lazily floated in the crystal clear deep, I thought of the very different experience of the day before. Which did I relish the most? Was it the spartan monk's cell and the Gregorian chant, or this hedonism? I concluded that I enjoyed both experiences in equal measure. It did, however, entail having both, not at the same time of course, but in pleasurable contrast.

Many weeks of solitary travel, coupled with my limited language skills, had left me starved of social contact. I felt so warmly embraced by the company on this beautiful island that I just had to stay for another day. My timetable was slipping all the while in this tranquil paradise.

One last swim and it was time to bid farewell to my new friends. Back on the bike on the long coastal road to Marseille, I focused on my reasons for choosing this way home. The main one, of course, was to experience a different return route, one that would not rejoin that of the outward journey until Paris. The second reason was that I wanted to see the Le Corbusier Unité d'habitation, a significant exemplar of post-war Modern Architecture.

When I reached the harbour of Marseille, I looked out to the bay beyond and saw a huge American aircraft carrier on the horizon. The vessel was apparently anchored way out, and it appeared as a two-dimensional, dark silhouette against the light. The stark horizontality of the flight deck fascinated me, but it was the slim vertical cluster of control tower and upper-works puncturing that strict horizontal line that made, for me, an almost perfect tableau of Modern Architecture. I was now eager to see Le Corbusier's latest work. I had no interest in the city of Marseille, finding it a grim and cheerless place, after all the bright towns on the Côte d'Azure.

I saw Unité d'habitation from far off, unmistakable and rising out of the ground like some giant white citadel. I had never seen anything like it and my enthusiasm for The Corb, as architectural students called him, was now unbounded. The façades were a rugged irregular mosaic of set-back balconies and light and shade. The whole structure sparkled in the sunshine. I was excited by the profile of the roof. Just like the aircraft carrier out in the bay, the almost mandatory element of Modern Architecture, the horizontal flat roof, was fretted against the skyline by a conglomeration of concrete shapes. Boiler flues, ventilator shafts, stairwell roof extensions and other structures were moulded in a variety of shapes to create an almost chaotic roof sculpture garden. As I wandered around this marvellous building, which was not yet occupied, excited thoughts and plans for my forthcoming thesis bubbled up.

It didn't take long for this enthusiasm to die away. I had a long journey up the Rhone valley and had little money left. How was I going to survive? The students on the island, knowing of my precarious finances, had given me a list of places on the way north that might, at least, solve some of my problems. This chain of youth hostels was funded by the French Communist Party and was called Amis de la Nature. They were free, they said, though a little primitive. I was getting well used to 'primitive'. The first one was just outside Marseille so I cycled off to find the address. I had a frustrating hour or so searching up and down squalid laneways, but eventually the dilapidated hostel appeared. The warden lived a few doors away and, without comment, he gave me the key. The building was untidy but reasonably clean, but for me its greatest asset was the kitchen shelves, lined with half-opened packets of food and even some unopened tins. I was alone because it seemed that the holiday season was long over. The bunk bed was comfortable enough and I went to sleep, well fed and a lot more optimistic that I would survive.

It was in Montelimar where I met the two Australian women. They were probably in their early thirties. I have no memory of the circumstances of our meeting. Maybe I was staring into a shop window at a display of mouth-watering boxes of nougat. Montelimar was apparently the world's capital for the production of that delicacy, as all the signs in the town announced. The women had, perhaps, been sitting outside a café enjoying their coffee when they saw this hungry-looking, scruffy youth gazing wistfully at this spectacle of luxury. I think that they must have invited me to join them at their table and I certainly remember that it was a delight to be able to speak English again. They were obviously intrepid travellers and some of the first long distance tourists in Europe, five years after the devastation of the war. My hostel was in the town and they invited me to have a meal with them later that evening. We shared our adventures and I was eternally grateful to them for their generosity. When I said farewell to them, and stood to return to the hostel, they presented me with a box of that delectable local nougat. I was overwhelmed by their gift and remember to this day my two Aussie good Samaritans.

Days went by as I moved up the Rhone valley – Valence, Vienne, Lyon – I remember names but little else of that lonely journey. The free hostels and scrounged food kept me going but my anxiety grew as I became aware of the distance still to be covered and I had now spent practically all my remaining francs.

It was somewhere just past the town of Macon that I found myself travelling through wine country. Long straight lines of vines, stretching into the distance, covered gentle slopes on both sides of the road. It then dawned on me that before I left for this journey to Rome, I had read about the French grape harvest and how it often offered the opportunity of casual jobs for pickers. Maybe this could be my salvation was my thought with quickening excitement. I could see people working on the lines quite far away, but then I came on a scene of bustling activity near the road. It was midday and the workers were leaving the lines of vines and crowding on to carts that began to trundle off up a long white laneway. They were heading to a scattering of farm buildings some distance away. I thought that this must be their midday break because surely they had been working since soon after first light. On an impulse I followed the carts until I came into a wide farmyard where all the workers were assembled. They looked at me with curiosity and when I began, in my limited French, to ask if I could have a job as a picker. I could see that they understood not a word and I could not grasp any of their dialect. There were friendly smiles all around, however, and I was invited to a bench and table where most were being seated.

A huge, steaming tureen was dumped on the table and soup was ladled out in bowls for everybody. The soup was thick and delicious; freshly baked bread was heaped unceremoniously along the wooden table and the feast began. I was in heaven. There was no rush to get back to work and the banter and laughter went on for more than an hour. I began to understand a few words and they, I thought, grasped a little of my story. I said I was Irish and that I had travelled to Rome and was on my way back to Paris and then Ireland. I'm not sure that they had ever heard about Ireland but they were impressed at my long cycle journey.

Finally people began to stand up. One man, who appeared to be the foreman, although his easy-going manner was not in any way authoritative, signalled for the horses to be harnessed up to the carts. He came up to me and indicated that I should park my *vélo* inside the open doors of a large barn and then jump up with the others on a cart. We were off: apparently I was hired. There was no mention of pay, or at least I didn't hear anything about it, but I didn't care; I was well fed and secure for the next few days.

I was placed with the pickers, almost all women, along with a handful of young children. The men had the task of walking up and down the lines of pickers, carrying shaped wicker baskets on their backs which were then gradually filled with the plucked grapes. These were brought to the carts and emptied into larger containers. From the start I loved the work: it was a huge change and a blessèd relief from the relentless pedaling day after day. The early October sunshine was still hot, but after weeks of much hotter days, I was happy with the task. There was something deeply satisfying in filling a container with the ripe fruit and straightening up to tilt the contents into the proffered basket and then the whole operation starts again. Nothing was rushed; a leisurely rhythm seemed to be the accepted way of working. There was lively chatter all along the lines and sometimes one person would break into song. I was enjoying it all but stayed silent because they often burst out laughing when I tried out my French. I ruefully considered this but knew full well that the laughter was good-humoured and that they enjoyed having me working with them.

In the late afternoon, everyone was relieved when we heard the foreman shout the words that were probably 'Time up'. Baskets and containers were emptied and we all piled on to the carts, now laden with grapes, and trundled back to the farm. A ritual developed here. The women all vanished into the farm kitchen while the men drove the carts into a large shed, lined with great wine barrels, where the contents were tumbled into a huge vat in the centre of the floor. Crumpled packets of Gauloises were handed around. I had not smoked for weeks – I couldn't afford to – and I greedily accepted a cigarette. The air in the shed was soon blue with smoke and the foreman now produced a tray of tiny glasses. The first enormous barrel was carefully tapped and each glass was filled with wine. We were all expected to taste and offer opinions on the various vintages. There were murmurs of appreciation as each vintage was tasted, but since I knew nothing about wine, I just gravely nodded my head as the others looked at me, for my approval or otherwise I supposed. I'm sure they knew I was bluffing but they were too polite to tease me.

The call came from the kitchen and everybody handed up their glasses. The foreman, I soon learned, was the owner of the farm and vineyard and his name was Jean. He and the others were already pronouncing my name as Jean. As I came out into the courtyard, Jean said to follow him, leading me to a large two-storey barn. We climbed up a steep wooden staircase into the upper floor, which was packed with hay. He pointed to a small bed, already made up, in a corner and, smiling, said that I could sleep here. As I followed him into the kitchen I couldn't believe my luck and how my perilous situation had been resolved.

The huge table was a sensation. I had never seen so much food or such a variety of dishes. Casseroles, tureens, pies, meat for carving, mountains of bread and, topping it all, dozens of wine bottles. The room was crowded with at least thirty people seated and others bustling around, setting out plates and glasses. When my plate was filled, I looked down, maybe a little confused. There were no knives or forks. My neighbour, seeing my hesitation, reached into his pocket and produced a clasp knife. Opening it, he wiped the blade on his trouser leg and, with a grin, handed me the implement. I was too hungry to be squeamish and tucked in as if starving. It was a feast, and with my wine glass being constantly refilled, the room seemed to revolve around me. The noise level rose, with a clamour of jokes, laughter and endless toasts, and although I understood hardly a word, I beamed inanely at every outbreak of mirth. A vague flash of memory: I am ascending the ancient wooden stairs to my hayloft bed, crawling on my hands and knees to a blissful state of oblivion.

An early October morning: I washed in icy cold water at the farmyard pump and, refreshed and alert, reported at the kitchen for breakfast. It was a much-depleted group that sat down at the enormous table. They were largely family members; the remaining workforce would join us later. I expected the usual French coffee and crusty bread, but in addition we were served a delicious omelette. My thought was that if this level of feasting went on, I would be too bloated to work. I felt that I was in seventh heaven; mindlessly boring days of cycling, half-starved, were behind me, replaced by this happy new circumstance.

That halcyon time was soon over, maybe four days, and I became anxious that my schedule was slipping away. I was certain to be very late for my college registration. I told Jean that I had to continue my journey and on the morning I left, shook hands with my co-workers and Jean handed me my pay. I thanked him and as I pedalled away, waved to the workforce, now back on the lines. It was joyful to see the forest of waving hands in reply.

My pay was modest, but the cornucopia of food, wine and my luxurious hayloft bed had made my journey's end not just satisfying but serene. I could now afford the official youth hostels all the way to Paris; I could buy food and, in a burst of reckless spending, I ate out one night at a restaurant. I also couldn't resist the temptation of roadside cafés where I sat outside and drank pastis, as every Frenchman seemed to do in the sunny mornings.

I rode into Paris long after dark, having spent the last of my francs that day. I pondered this as I cycled along the nearly deserted streets. I now had only one option and that was to cycle through the night and hope to catch the next day's boat from Dieppe. Having made the decision to ride on, I felt the anxiety about my renewed parlous finances fade away, to be replaced by a burst of optimism that journey's end was now in sight. I cycled strongly for several hours but became increasingly drowsy. Suddenly I found myself sprawled on the grass verge. I had tumbled off the bike, being overcome by sleep. There was a sickle moon but in a blaze of starlight I saw the dark outline of what was an old haystack in the field opposite. I wheeled my bike behind the stack and out of sight from the road. I knew that I just had to sleep, for a few hours, at least.

It was the cold that wakened me. It was still several hours before dawn, the moon was low in the sky and long grasses were speckled white with early frost. I got back on the road and the numbing cold revived me. I was now riding more strongly and eating up the miles. The first light of dawn saw me in Normandy when I passed through a forest of apple trees on both sides of the highway. The grass verges were covered with masses of fallen fruit. I stopped to pick some of the unbruised specimens and filled my panniers, satisfied that I now had food for the journey. When I rolled on to quayside of Dieppe I had less that thirty minutes to spare. It was a huge relief to relax in the ship's lounge and buy an ice cream with part of my remaining single pound note.

When I arrived in London, I cycled straight to Euston Station, with my return ticket, to catch the night train to Holyhead. I must have slept for most of that train journey. I went out on the mail boat deck in the early morning and saw the misty grey outline of the Wicklow Mountains along the western horizon. My first thought was: am I triumphant at the end of my epic journey? In truth, my only real feeling was that I was glad it was over.

I went into college the very next day. I was now about eight days late for registration into the fifth and final year of the course. As I expected, I was reprimanded for my lateness, but, perhaps because of my more senior status, the strictures were perfunctory. Our fifth-year studio was tucked away at the end of the main Earlsfort Terrace building at the Hatch Street end. The only significant feature I remember that small space had was a cast iron stove, with a large coalbunker alongside. There were only seventeen of us in that final year, so the studio was a cosy and sequestered place, well suited for our lofty standing. Most of us, though, spent little time in the studio, preferring to do most of our drawing work at home. I have one memory of a bitterly cold winter morning, when I happened to be working at my bench with the stove keeping the place snugly warm. Two fellow final year students came in carrying briefcases that they calmly filled to almost bursting point with coal from the bunker. This operation was swift and they were gone in minutes, back to their lodgings in Harrington Street. They told us that the room they shared in the 'digs' was miserably cold and damp.

My thesis was Dun Laoghaire harbour, with a modern mail boat pier and other new waterside buildings. I had always been fascinated by the sweep of the great enfolding granite piers, the sheer muscularity of the carved stone blocks of walls and walkways and, particularly, by the massive breakwater of giant fractured boulders. I couldn't wait to draw all those seductive elements. I worked on my drawings at home, my drawing board perched, sometimes precariously, on my sofa bed. It was chancing fate to attempt to transport my double elephant board, with an unfinished drawing, on my motorbike to college; I had another board in the studio and carried drawings rolled securely in a cardboard tube. This was a wise decision as it turned out.

After the thesis was finished and approved, we had a few final subject examinations. It must have been on the last of these days that near disaster struck. I crashed my motor bike on the Stillorgan Road on my way into the exam hall in Earlsfort Terrace. I skidded when a van in front of me braked suddenly and I slid along the road on my back, fortunately separated from the bike. I was bruised and had a few superficial cuts; the bike was not badly damaged but the handlebars were bent and one footrest had broken off, so I couldn't ride it safely. Propping the bike against a wall, I managed to catch a bus into town fairly quickly. It was just in time before the exam doors were closed. There was no space to clean up and I had to be careful not to get blood on my answer paper. It was an easy exam for me, for which I was greatly relieved.

Unlike the memory of the impersonal and uncaring way of announcing our first-year exam results, an occasion I remembered so well, I have no memory of how I received my own final result. I recall only the celebrations. Inevitably these must have begun in Hartigan's, around the corner from college, but memory is blurred. Five long years of student life were over, with no thought of the future; there was only the moment. I have one distinct memory: walking on Killiney beach long after dark on that balmy June night. We were a small group of fellow new graduates and one of us had borrowed a car. It was well after midnight when I was deposited at my gateway in Woodside.

There was a light on in the kitchen and when I walked in, a little unsteadily, my parents were still sitting at the fireside. They looked at me expectantly. 'I passed,' I said. The relief on their faces was palpable. They smiled as I said goodnight. In truth, the highs of that historic day were waning and all I needed now was sleep.

I lost little time that summer in finding a new job. I was hired by Michael Scott, a practice that was highly favoured by young architects. Before I started my first day's work at the famous office at 19 Merrion Square, I called on Desmond FitzGerald and told him that I would not be coming back to him because I had a new place. At first he said he was sorry that I was leaving him, because he hoped I would rejoin the practice when I qualified, but he said that he quite understood that I wanted a change. His manner grew dark, however, when I said that it was in Michael Scott's office. There were many divisions and even enmities between architectural offices in those competitive and sometimes cutthroat days. Fitz did not speak to me for many years after this exchange. When I interviewed him then, for a research project of mine, he was an old man, long retired. He was genial, garrulous and spoke to me as if we were long-lost friends.

My time in No. 19 was a happy one and was also deeply satisfying for a young architect. The workforce was treated as a team with little feeling of hierarchy. The pay was good, as good if not better than most other offices, particularly for me, recently qualified. I bought a new motorbike – the old BSA had been scrapped – the latest post-war German model, an NSU Lux. In contrast to the full-throated roar of the 500cc, ex-military bike, the Lux engine was a genteel buzzing. I did at times miss the earsplitting bellow of my old BSA.

I had my first Alpine season in the summer of 1952. We were a small team – Brendan, Frank and me – and we went to the Austrian Tyrol. We had each read *Over Tyrolese Hills* (1936) by the celebrated mountaineer and writer Frank Smythe. His sumptuous black and white photographs of those mountains inspired us, and the book became our guide for those superb peaks. It was a highly successful climbing trip and the three of us were cock-a-hoop at our new status as alpinists. In the winter of that year the Irish Mountaineering Club resumed its indoor meets, as they were called, where members could share their stories of summer expeditions. The most important element of these gatherings was the showing of slides of mountain adventures. The clubrooms were in Ely Place and it was there, on one of the earliest winter evenings, that Nuala Carey walked into my life.

She and two friends had come as prospective new members and to learn about this new sport. I was immediately attracted to the nineteen-year-old who moved with a grace that spoke of energy and awareness. I did fall in love at that moment but, unlike my seventeen-year-old self where I didn't know it, I knew it this time deep down, but could not say the words then or for a long time. Over the next few weeks I set out with determination to woo Nuala. At first we went out in group mountain walks, but I soon managed to persuade her to come with me to one of my favourite high and wild places, the valley above Powerscourt waterfall in the Wicklow mountains.

My arrival on a motorbike to pick her up, at her home on Parnell Road, caused quite a sensation. Nuala told me this later: her mother had considerable anxiety about her safety as a pillion passenger. Nuala herself had some apprehension when she saw the mountains ahead covered in snow. From the Rocky Valley the roads were slippery and we soon had to abandon the bike and walk on to the base of Maulin. A meandering track led out to the wide open mountain wilderness. It was here at the edge of the forest that I found a shallow grassy hollow that was almost snow-free and sheltered from the wind. The sun was shining on that early spring day as we settled down for a midday lunch stop. I began to make a little fire, first gathering clumps of dry moss and twigs and then building a pyramid of slightly thicker sticks over the tinder dry core, which I lit with one match. We soon had a cosy fire going and Nuala was highly impressed. I felt deeply satisfied that I had demonstrated my bushman skills, and the signs were good that the courtship was progressing.

After that first date we spent most weekends together, rock-climbing in Glendalough, on the sun-warmed granite cliffs of Camaderry or walking in the Wicklow Mountains. Camping trips to Donegal, Connemara or Kerry became a feature of longer weekends or holidays. Nuala and I began to share a tent. She later said that she was always mystified as to why her parents, both strait-laced Catholics, accepted this arrangement for their daughter because they had habitually railed against her staying out late on a date. I said that this was because they thought that camping in the cold outdoors was an obviously uncomfortable experience, and therefore must be healthily virtuous. Little did they know! I had bought a double sleeping bag from Blacks, the Scottish sports shop, and we were able to keep warm and snug on winter nights out there in the healthy outdoors.

Our first holiday together was a climbing expedition to Scotland and the island of Skye. The Black Cuillins were one of the great attractions for all serious mountaineers and I for one could not wait to see them. It was an exhilarating motorcycle ride up through the Scottish Highlands on a glorious sunny day. We were too late for the evening ferry – the bridge had not yet been built – so we had to check into the local hotel. Unmarried couples could be refused the sharing of a hotel room in those days, so buying a cheap gold wedding ring was the usual subterfuge. I think we were both too naïve to think of that possibility before this, our first holiday as a couple. I took a chance and asked for a room, and to my surprise and delighted anticipation, I was handed a key and we had our first experience of the pleasure of sharing a double bed all night long.

It was very different in Mrs. Campbell's cottage the next morning. We had made our booking for this famous climbing venue in Glen Brittle some months before, and in both our names. There would be no hanky panky allowed by the redoubtable Mrs. Campbell. She welcomed us warmly but firmly and pointedly showed Nuala to a bedroom next door to her own. When my turn came, I found that I was banished to a room in an extension, as far away as possible from my beloved girlfriend. Nocturnal wanderings were still possible, however, but these had to be stealthy: maybe these adventures were even more exciting, for me at least, than our rock-climbing.

We had nearly eight blissful days on those enchanting peaks with only one huge thunderstorm that nearly wiped us from a long rock route to the left of the famous *Srón*. The most memorable day was a long walk around the edge of the Cuillins to a remote sea inlet. We spent hours in that wild and lovely place.

Mrs. Campbell not only attempted to keep us on the straight and narrow path, thus avoiding the temptations of the flesh, she was also adamant that the Sabbath was sacrosanct. No earthly pleasures were to be indulged in from her establishment on the seventh day, and this included mountain climbing. With all that, she was a warm and kindly person and looked after us like a mother and she could enjoy a joke as much as anyone.

We said farewell on our last morning and thanked her for a wonderful stay and then sped away to catch the early ferry. When we rode into the wide expanse of Glencoe the sky to the west was darkly menacing and we felt the first stings of rain. Away in the distance we could see the black and white cluster of the ancient Kings House Hotel, huddled under and dominated by the towering Buchaille Etive Mór, still streaked with winter snow. This had been a famous place for climbers since the early days of Scottish mountaineering and I wanted to see it. The weather got worse, so it promised shelter.

Our stay with Mrs. Campbell had left us with a sense of probity, rectitude even, so at reception we asked for two separate rooms. The young receptionist brought us upstairs and ushered Nuala into a large room with a dormer window, and an enormous double bed. I stayed at the door, waiting to be shown to my room while gazing longingly at that bed. The receptionist beckoned me to come in and showed me a tiny alcove off the huge room, the only furniture being a narrow single bed. 'This is your room,' she said and left us with a knowing smile. I don't know why I found it necessary to rumple up the bedclothes of that single bed the next morning.

The solution to our moral dilemma was inevitable. I don't remember where the actual words were spoken; it might have been on one of the sandy beaches of south Wicklow or Wexford or, more likely, when we were snuggled up in our sleeping bag in a tent in the mountains, but it was a simple solution. We got engaged.

Nuala and I married on 7 February 1956. Members of the Irish Mountaineering Club formed an arch of ice axes as we walked out of the church on Clogher Road. The reception was held at Nuala's home, facing the Grand Canal. Our honeymoon was to be spent in the Zetland Hotel in Connemara and initially we planned, or at least I did, to travel there on my motorbike. This proposal was met with incredulity and dismissed by family members as ill-advised. A kind friend offered the loan of a car and we set off for the West of Ireland.

Shortly after we left, we had to stop and cut off the cacophony of empty cans tied to the rear bumper. We hoped the confetti still clinging to the roof would blow away as we picked up speed. All went well until some distance before Kilbeggan when, on a bend in the road, there was a loud bang. I lost control of the steering as the car ran on to the grass verge and stopped with a thump against a low stone wall. I got out to view the damage and saw that one of the front tires had burst but the wheel was now badly dented and it would not be possible to fit the spare tire.

We stood on the verge wondering what to do, when a large lorry, filled with sheep, pulled up beside us. The driver leaned out and asked could he give us a lift to the next village where there was a garage. We climbed into the cab and he remarked, 'I see ye were married this morning, I'm getting married myself tomorrow.' Our car was still speckled with confetti. He paused at the garage in the nearby village and I arranged for the car to be towed in and the wheel repaired. The lorry driver then said that he would bring us on to Athlone where we could take the train to Galway. We thanked our benefactor when he dropped us off at the station and wished him well for his own wedding in the morning.

The last train for Galway had left, so we checked into the nearest hotel. Before we retired, now fairly exhausted, I first phoned our friend and told her about the car. She told us not to worry but to go on and enjoy the honeymoon. We both thanked her and, vastly relieved, I called the Zetland to explain our dilemma. They were immediately sympathetic and said they would send a car to meet us at Galway station and take us to our hotel. We were overwhelmed by all the benevolence offered to us after the disastrous start to our honeymoon.

The car was waiting for us just outside the station. The driver smilingly greeted us and placed our bags into the boot. We felt like royalty. After the town of Oughterard the landscape changed utterly. A panorama of wild moorland, stark mountains and lakes opened up and the vast expanse of sky made for a scene of breathtaking beauty. The narrow road down to the hotel snaked, swerved and undulated past huge boulders and heathery hillocks, until the gleam of the sea ahead promised an end to the jolting and dizziness of the drive. The hotel sat in a small oasis of tall fir trees and spindly birches, and the gardens opened up to the almost land-locked Bertraghboy

Bay. The manager greeted us and showed us to our room, a luxurious space with a window looking out to a sunlit seascape. That stunning view, however, was momentarily eclipsed by the spectacle of the twin beds. Did they not appreciate the significance of our being newlyweds?

I remember that we had our first married tiff there and then. Nuala felt that it was my job to demand a room with a double bed while I thought that we should both undertake this delicate task. A compromise was quickly reached: we both agreed that it was an exceptionally lovely room and the solution was just to push the two beds close together.

Before early darkness we went out to explore the gardens. Outcrops of living rock randomly pushed up from the well-cropped grass lawns, thus easily moulding into the surrounding wild nature. Green spears of daffodils were the first signs of early spring, along with clusters of snowdrops under the silver birches. We assumed that we were the only guests in the hotel that night, but when we went into dinner we met our only other fellow diners, an elderly clergyman and his wife. They asked us to join them after the meal, the four of us retiring to the lounge for coffee. When they heard our story of the mishap with the car, and the loss of our transport for the next two weeks, they immediately offered to take us each day to wherever we wanted and would meet us after our walk to bring us back to the hotel. The benevolence that had overpowered us this honeymoon seemed endless and we accepted their wonderful offer at once.

Day after day the pattern was the same. Booted and well clad for the outdoors, we bundled into the rear seat of their old Ford and were deposited at the starting point for our walk or climb. The afternoon pick-up place and time were prearranged and we never had to wait when we arrived at the finish, because the kind couple were always there before us.

We climbed Ben Corr on one splendid day of stillness when all around us the peaks were sharp-etched, summits dusted with snow. As we descended the steep northern side, we could see, on the far distant road through Glen Inagh, the tiny dark shape of our Good Samaritans' car. It took us almost an hour to cross the flat expanse of bogland but when we reached the Ford they, as always, greeted us with the friendliest of smiles.

Memories of those bygone days in Connemara are fragmentary but every imagined image is richly remembered. We walked along the banks of the silk-flowing, amber dark waters of the Owengowla River, and on another day strode the white sands of Gurteen Bay and on to the grassy headland that faced out to the open ocean. I have no memory that we discussed our future or anything other than that there were just the two us, living in the moment. On our last day we climbed Erris Beg. This stand-alone little peak stood sentinel at the edge of a bewildering matrix of glittering lakelets, a scene of half-water, half-land stretching out to the west.

We made love on top of that mountain. Three months later we were living and working in Africa, but that's another story.

Epilogue

I have a recurring dream. My father is driving me down a country lane. Ahead, mature trees on both sides of the roadway are arching over to form a canopy. We are entering a green tunnel and sometimes there is daylight at the end but often the dream fades as we drive down that tunnel. I still recall the dream whenever I find myself driving along a road where the trees overhang on both sides to form a green roof. I have no memory that this was an actual event. I do, however, have vivid memories of other outings with my father when I was young. I could not have been more than three or four when he took me to a football match. He was always a fan of Shamrock Rovers and their home ground was in Milltown. I am at the edge of the field, before the game, being asked to kick the ball. Was I a mascot for the team? I don't know, but I can still picture the scene: a joyous one for sure.

A flicker of memory: I am on a beach; an aeroplane is moving off down the sand and then floating up into the sky. Did it happen? The first east to west solo transatlantic flight was in 1932 and it took off from Portmarnock Strand. I was there – at four years old in that year – so this must have been another adventure with my father. Sometime in the late 1930s he took me out to Greystones in County Wicklow after a great storm had deeply eroded the coast at that seaside village. I remember the extraordinary sight of cottages being smashed by the waves, now far out in an encroaching sea. After the Luftwaffe bombed the North Strand in Dublin, how could my father resist the desire to see that destruction for himself? He had an abiding curiosity, as well as a huge hunger, for new things. There were many other occasions, all when I was very young, when my father and I had trips together. I was the first-born, after all, so this singular treatment was only natural. There was, perhaps, a special bond between my father and me, at least in my very early years. This relationship would change, however, as I grew older.

I have only one memory of my father playing with us as children in those far-off days. It might have been a Sunday morning. It was a highly exciting game that consisted of my father chasing us around the garden shouting 'Hula, Hula, Hula' as we tried to hide behind the fruit bushes. I also remember well the disappointment when sometimes he abruptly left and we did not see him for the rest of the day. Whenever I talked about my father in later years, and this was seldom, I always remarked, 'He was never there.' In the summer during the pre-war years he would occasionally drive the family out to Bray. Our car was always a Ford: he would say about Fords, 'You could repair them with a hammer.' When he parked the car, we all trooped down to the beach but then he would vanish for most of the afternoon, leaving us with our mother. He was attracted to the 'Amusements': slot machine establishments that lined the rear of the promenade. He would, however, always bring us each an ice cream cone when he came to collect us.

During those early years when his various projects were successful, his favourite evening and night recreation place was the Red Bank restaurant and bar in the centre of Dublin. He would take my mother with him for a while but later took to going alone and often staying out late. As I grew a little older, I became aware of tensions between my parents. My mother would stay up waiting for him to come home. There was little traffic in those years and I would often lie awake listening for the sound of his car climbing up Slate Cabin Lane. Then the voices would begin, gradually rising until one night I got out of bed and rushed into the living room where a row was in progress. The shouting stopped when I appeared and raised my fists to my father. I was about thirteen or fourteen. I remember the look on his face when I told him to stop. I think we began to draw apart from that night on.

My father's entrepreneurial skills seem to desert him in the years after World War II. He had a series of business failures and I think he began to lose heart; those years in Ireland were bleak in any case and most of the vigour and optimism that were once his strengths seemed to fade away. I don't think that I really forgave him, in my mind at least, for his virtual abandonment of our family. It took a long time for me to soften my attitude to him and to realise that my own censure of his behaviour was self-righteous and judgmental. When Nuala and I returned after three years in Africa in the late 1950s, my father had disappeared. We found that he had gone to Liverpool, as many Irish people had done in those depressing years, a time of despair and hopelessness for him and for other emigrants.

I went to look for him, in that same ship where emigrants shared the voyage with cattle. These animals were packed in the hold and exported for slaughter in England. I remember little of that trip: facts became a blur in my memory of the search. At the end I found him in a Salvation Army hostel. He was old and ill, long before his time, but we managed to get him home. I have one clear and happy memory of his last days. He is sitting in our family house in Woodside, smiling while he cradled his second grandchild, Colm, in his arms. He died of cancer in 1961 in Hume Street Hospital, aged sixty-four. I was with him when he died. I embraced his shrunken shoulders and told him that I loved him. He faintly smiled and then he left us.

My father had a military funeral: an honour he earned as a prominent Old IRA man. The night before the funeral, my brother Eamon and I helped to carry his coffin into the little church in Sandyford village. My younger brother Brian was in Canada and could not get back in time. I remember little of that church ceremony except that it was packed with friends, relatives and local people from the Barnacullia and Glencullen neighbourhoods. I have, however, a vivid memory of the burial. The hearse drove up from the gates of the Dean's Grange Cemetery, the military party slow-marching behind with the coffin, now draped in the national flag. My mother, brother Eamon, his wife Marie, sister Isobel, Nuala and I were next after the soldiers. It was barely two years since, side by side with Nuala, I had carried the tiny white coffin of our baby son, Niall Peter, up that short path into the cemetery in Kampala. I knew that in that moment Nuala and I, yet again, both felt the grief of that morning in the African sunshine.

The prayers at the graveside were brief and the officer in charge gave the order to the firing party. Three volleys splintered the silence and then, with the heart-breaking sound of the Last Post, it was impossible to hold back the tears. The tricolour was removed from the coffin, carefully folded by two soldiers, and the officer solemnly presented it to my mother. The empty shells of the spent bullets were collected and presented to my brother Eamon, sister Isobel and me.

I remember my father now, with regret and sometimes real sorrow that we grew so far apart. I often think of him as I drive alone and the sharing we might have had if driving together: of cars, perhaps, or roads, or about anything, but particularly that green tunnel of the past.